Better Behaviour in Classrooms

Better Behaviour in Classrooms provides a professional and sympathetic approach to the difficulties presented by disruptive behaviour, and offers a range of tried and tested strategies to help teachers develop a whole-school approach to behaviour management.

By drawing on their considerable experiences of dealing with children's emotional and behavioural difficulties, the authors acknowledge existing good practice and seek to build on it, showing how every teacher can improve their skills through a planned and stepped programme. The book provides a practical overview of whole-school behavioural patterns and a detailed focus on individual classroom interactions, explaining how prediction skills can be used to plan an effective behaviour management strategy.

The book also includes helpful photocopiable resources and training materials for use with staff groups or individuals. It is an invaluable resource for all newly-qualified and established teachers concerned about behaviour. Head teachers, senior-management teams and advisory teachers will also find it an excellent basis for the delivery of whole-school INSET courses.

Kay Mathieson is a Senior Teacher at a Pupil Referral Unit. **Meg Price** is a Principal Teacher in an inner-city secondary school.

Better Behaviour in Classrooms

A framework for inclusive behaviour management

Kay Mathieson and Meg Price

London and New York

First published 2002 by RoutledgeFalmer
11 New Fetter Lane, London EC4P 4EE

Simultaneously published in the USA and Canada
by RoutledgeFalmer
29 West 35th Street, New York, NY 10001

RoutledgeFalmer is an imprint of the Taylor & Francis Group

Typeset in Sabon and Gill Sans by Exe Valley Dataset Ltd, Exeter
Printed and bound in Great Britain by
TJ International Ltd, Padstow, Cornwall

British Library Cataloguing in Publication Data
A catalogue record for this book is available from the British Library

Library of Congress Cataloging in Publication Data
A catalog record for this book has been requested.

ISBN 0–415–25341–1

Contents

Introduction   1

1   Communicating with the emotional brain   3

2   From policy to practice: Consensus behaviour management within
    the institution   7

3   The Big Picture: Behavioural patterns in the academic year   15

4   Consensus-driven behaviour planning within the classroom   20

5   Behaviour – taught not caught, making the message clear   24

6   Managing the emotional environment in the classroom   28

7   Managing the physical environment in the classroom   33

8   The reflective practitioner: Considering the whole class
    environment   36

9   Consolidation phase: Considering behaviour from the
    pupils' perspective   41

10 Transitions: Identifying areas of increased concern   49

11 Planning spirit lifters: Incentives for good behaviour   52

    Conclusion: The role of the teacher   55

INSET Sessions   58

    Communicating with the emotional brain   61

  Theme: Authority   68

    Session 1   *Authority – a dirty word?*   69

    Activity 1   *Authority – seeking a working definition*   69
    Summary 1   72

    Session 2   *Styles of conflict management – the
                        collaborative model*   73

    Activity 2   *Making the intervention count*   77
    Summary 2   80

    Session 3   *Characteristics of the authoritative teacher* 81

    Activity 3   *Am I insulated against role strain?*   81
    Summary 3   *A personal audit*   82

  Theme: Behaviour issues   85

    Session 1   *Behaviour as an issue*   86

    Activity 1a   *What's the worst thing?*   86
    Activity 1b   *Moderating decisions*   87

    Session 2   *The establishment phase – laying the
                        foundations*   89

    Activity 2a   *How would we like it to be?*   89
    Activity 2b   *The behaviour management framework*   91

    Session 3   *Consolidation phase – making the most
                        of it*   93

    Activity 3a   *Reframing our view of behaviour*   93
    Activity 3b   *Building strategies*   93

    Session 4   *Transition phase – dealing with the anxieties* 94

    Activity 4a   *Coping with change*   94
    Activity 4b   *Easing the change process*   94

Suggested further reading   95

Index   96

Dedication

For Vi Ritchie – She knows why

Acknowledgements

Thanks to Helen Roberts for her wonderfully quirky illustrations (pod.roberts@btinternet.com). Thanks to Simone, for her influence and guidance. Thanks to Tricia for her support in clarifying ideas, to staff members of Acorn House and Victoria House pupil referral units, and to Alison and the staff of the EBD unit at St Machar Academy – you have all showed us more about commitment and team work than we could have imagined. Thanks to Nora who helped us believe we could produce this book. Thanks to James for his continued support, constructive help and his typing expertise. Thanks to Will, Alex and Jessi for their cheerful encouragement. Thanks to our families who have enabled us to maintain a positive approach to the challenges of life.

Introduction

ALL IN THE SAME BOAT?

It has been said that trying to effect change in educational practice is like 'sailing in a stormy sea in a leaky boat with a mutinous crew'. Difficult, dangerous, and presumably doomed to a watery grave! If we, as teachers, are to hold up our hands as a mutinous crew, we can at least be forgiven for posing a few questions about the leaky boat. The issue of behaviour management, in particular trying to promote inclusive behaviour, is fundamentally an emotional one, and is ill-served by a coercive approach.

The management of our pupils is a very personal matter. We invest a great deal more of ourselves, as people, into this than into any of the other elements of good pedagogy. The risk we take is a very public one, our management style and the behaviour of our pupils can be viewed by many other people.

The behaviour of students generates more passion at coffee time than just about any other aspect of education. The views we, as individuals, are willing to share in this situation are, of course, affected by the response we anticipate from colleagues.

In this book we have sought to acknowledge the difficulties that present in the management of the behaviour in our schools and classrooms. As practitioners we are aware of, and sympathetic to, mounting concerns over behaviour as an issue in education. The pragmatic and strategic approach we offer has been tried and tested over years both in mainstream and in off-site provision.

If, as a profession, we can accept that the behaviour we require in our classroom can be taught, then we can apply our skills to behaviour, as we would in any other area of the curriculum. Behaviour as an issue can have the effect of polarising staff rooms, it can dishearten, distress and demoralise, as well as generating much ribald cynicism and thumping good 'war stories'.

So much of our self-belief as teachers comes from our confidence in our ability to manage the youngsters in front of us. It's clear, then, that if change is needed in our practice, it will only be achieved by enhancing that self-belief.

There is something incongruous in the notion that we can promote positive and optimistic regimes by anything other than positive and optimistic measures. We are unlikely to reduce exclusions by being told that we must, by being set targets and mandatory quotas. Such an approach is very likely to unite us as a profession, but more on emotional than rational grounds.

We see the stories in the press where a hapless youngster, having been excluded from every school in the authority, is paraded about by indignant parents crying 'foul'. We look at the picture of newly-scrubbed butter wouldn't melt innocence . . . and are not deceived! Up and down the country, teachers are instantly united in a surge of professional fellow-feeling.

We are also sympathetic to the school when an exclusion is overturned by a local authority or a board of governors. Aware as we are, that allowing a pupil to remain on the school premises, to the chagrin of many of the staff, will do little for teacher morale and perhaps as importantly, absolutely nothing for that pupil's education – and is nothing whatsoever to do with inclusion. We will reduce exclusions only by actively promoting inclusive behaviour, which would seem to be a truism, but in fact is much more to do with finding and sharing a consensus of purpose and by developing our expertise in the management of behaviour in order to drive that consensus.

Every school is a unique community, not a commodity. Schools must look for solutions that are congruent to the particular needs of all the stakeholders within that community – the route to inclusion begins with that search. The teaching staff of any school is acknowledged as its greatest resource, and it is absolutely vital for teachers to feel confident and empowered in order to tackle the stresses of the job in an optimistic, vigorous and completely professional manner.

The in-set section of this book explores the behavioural challenges teachers encounter on a daily basis, and provides a repertoire of skills and strategies to address them.

1 Communicating with the emotional brain

COMMUNICATING WITH THE EMOTIONAL BRAIN – LESSON ONE!

Human interaction is a very complex process, as yet not completely understood. Our communication skills are central to our teaching equipment and it is important to have some understanding of the factors influencing the communication process. Recent research into the way the human brain functions proclaims the futility of an overtly coercive punishment-based regime.

Every human being is in possession of a three-part triune brain. The diagram shows the processes involved in each area of the three-part brain. In times of difficulty or threat the blood flow follows the direction of the arrow to the left of the diagram. The effect is that the reptilian brain is the active part during such times. The 'thinking' part (neo-cortex) is therefore unable to have significant influence on the situation.

The three-part (triune) brain

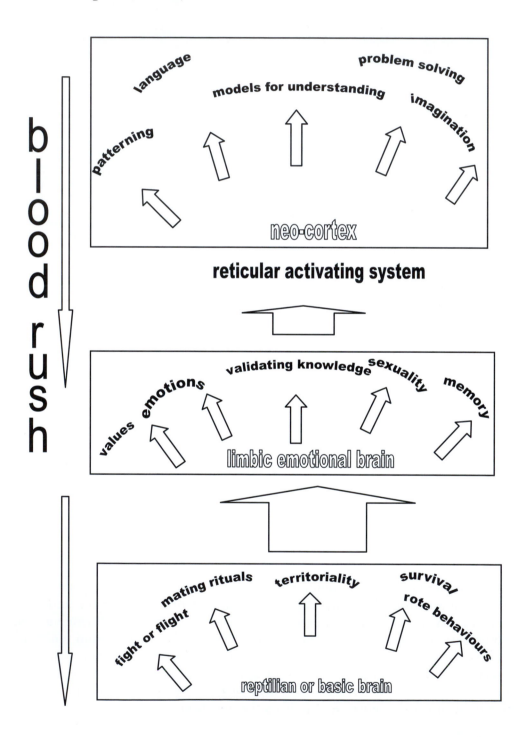

The basic (reptilian) brain

The reptilian brain governs our primitive responses and survival instincts of:

- Fight or flight
- Defence of territory.

As this is instinctive, there is no conscious control. If the brain perceives a threat, whether physical, emotional or indeed real, the blood supply retreats from the limbic and neo-cortex brain to fuel the reptilian brain. Anecdotally we are aware of 'the rush of blood' and 'the adrenalin rush' in such situations. Other physiological changes take place in the body at the same time, and we become aware of an increased heart and breathing rate, and of the blood pounding in our ears. When this response is aroused, the other parts of the brain are unable to function until the stress has subsided or has been resolved.

The limbic system (emotional brain)

Above the reptilian brain is found the emotional brain (limbic system) which governs memory values and obviously our emotions. This part of the brain provides much of the blue-print that makes each of us unique, a distillation of all our experiences, conditioning and stimuli.

Sitting on top of the emotional brain is something called the reticular activating system (RAS) which acts as a filter to the neo-cortex, only allowing through that which resonates with the emotional 'mind-map', or appears to be personally relevant. Communicating with the emotional brain is the critical and fundamental feature of our dealings with each other as human beings – in order to prevent rousing the reptilian brain, but also to allow the neo cortex to become engaged in order for learning to take place.

The neo-cortex governs the higher order skills – the right and left brain functions such as language, logic, patterns and sequences, recognition and imagination. Because the brain responds in this rather hierarchical way it effectively shuts down the neo cortex if the reptilian or limbic systems predominate.

A learner who is feeling insecure and threatened, undervalued or ignored and powerless will find it very difficult to operate as a thinking person. If this sounds in any way familiar, it should, as it describes how a significant number of us in this profession feel when faced by hostile and disruptive students and/or their hostile and disruptive parents. We are just as vulnerable as our pupils, because our brains naturally function in exactly the same way, and our self-esteem is just as much at stake as theirs.

The ways in which we seek to bolster our self-esteem are crucial, however, and must be characterised by the calm expertise that we try to describe in subsequent chapters. We can in fact, translate the emotional needs of the learner into two fairly simple questions:

1   What am I supposed to be doing?
- I need the 'big picture' so I can see where I'm going and then I can accept a variety of pathways

- I need to share the worth of the purpose
- I need regular feedback and constant reminders
- I need to see how much progress I'm making
- I need to establish routines and familiar patterns.

2   How am I getting on?
- I need genuine encouragement, to be told when I'm getting it right to increase my confidence and keep me going
- I need to experience approval and some success
- I need to know where I'm going wrong, to be given helpful criticism and reminders of when I've got it right
- I need targets to be identified so that I can see how far I have come

Teachers, as learners, have the same emotional needs as every other learner. These two questions hold good for anyone trying to effect any change of practice involving emotional issues, such as behaviour management. The route to change begins by acknowledging this and would indicate a measured and incremental process, beginning with the search for consensus of purpose. This consensus will prove the vital element in the process of energising commitment and honing the skills of a critical mass of the school's staff.

This sharing of the purpose begins with the school's discipline policy which we will consider in detail in Chapter 2.

2   From policy to practice

Consensus behaviour management within the institution

© Helen Roberts

Every school is required by law to have a written policy to dot every i and cross every t. For many of us, the various policies represent an internal response to external pressures, whether from the government, the local authority, or society at large. This may not suit the school's discipline policy particularly well. For this policy to be germane and effective, it must be informed by the nature of the institution and the needs and aspirations of all the stakeholders therein, which must include teachers, parents, pupils, and non-teaching staff, as well as the local authority.

The initial process of developing the policy requires a lot of discussion to clarify viewpoints and definitions around behaviour. It should involve the development of a common understanding of the meanings and implications of behavioural issues for the specific establishment.

The document produced from the initial process is the culmination of many hours of blood, sweat and tears. It is often evidence of personal conflict and compromise. The annual revision of the document however, is not always subject to such scrutiny. The result can be that it does not reflect the changes in staff, pupils, parents and the wider society context. We can then be in danger of attempting to address today's behaviours with yesterday's strategies. The current document should be there to support all stakeholders in their understanding of the behaviour issues. It should be a means to establish a common currency of the rewards and sanctions which maintain the community of the school.

There are dangers inherent in putting together a discipline policy if no cognisance is to be taken of the fact that we are trying to operate that policy very firmly in the emotional zone. Check lists, punishment tariffs and sanctions may sit uneasily with the intention to promote positive and optimistic classroom regimes. This is in no way to deny the need for a tightly structured regime – check lists and tariffs and the sanctions available to us provide all the stakeholders with a sense of security. There is comfort in the belief that we are operating in a well-ordered establishment, indeed the opposite produces great stress and anxiety for staff and pupils alike.

The essence of any discipline policy must encompass the legitimate expect-ations and aspirations of everyone involved to be viable. A discipline policy therefore cannot be a 'one-off' document, a tablet of stone that will remain in perpetuity. Rather it must be a document constantly revised to meet changing demands. It is well understood that a school is a community, but we need to be realistic about the changing nature of that community. This transience is often underestimated. A policy, once committed to paper, takes on a permanence which may not be useful. Every year, in fact, the nature of the school can change, from the loss of senior students to the calibre and constitution of the new intake, as well as changes in the teaching staff, budget, etc.

A discipline policy on paper may have no power to drive the regime in reality, nor is it of much value for us to shelter under in our daily dealings with our pupils, unless it provides useful strategic day-to-day survival techniques for teachers to hold on to. Once in place, therefore, every opportunity must be taken to bring the policy off the paper and into the corridors and classrooms. It must also provide answers to the questions 'What am I supposed to be doing?' and 'How am I getting on?' This should be particularly true for the two major stakeholders of pupils/parents and staff.

For staff, the policy can provide the basis for:

- a sharing of purpose, this revision of the agreed principles and practice on a regular basis encourages communication of common aims

- in-service and staff development
- acknowledgement of the difficulties teachers will encounter and specific support which is available
- modelling of good practice through consistency of approach and clear indicators about use of rewards and sanctions as well as strategies available
- support for inexperienced staff communicating elements of best practice
- opportunity to share anxieties in a supportive framework
- a set of guidelines for staff to inform practice
- a 'survival' guide for temporary/supply staff, this needs to communicate the essence of the document and a quick reference to rewards and sanctions required on a daily basis
- 'pats on the back' – recognition of good practice.

For pupils and their parents the policy can provide the basis for:

- a sharing of purpose and clear communication of the principles which inform practice within the school
- modelling of required behaviour
- acknowledgement of the difficulties which may occur and how they will be resolved
- support available and how it can be obtained
- 'pats on the back' acknowledgement of positive contributions of all stakeholders and their effectiveness.

Many elements of the policy can be enforced without equivocation, use of mobile phones, smoking, truancy, timekeeping and uniform, for example are well served by clearly delineated policy statements. Not many arguments against these statements are likely to be credible, nor are they likely to be contested by a combative response from pupil or parent, since they are likely to have agreed with these elements on entry to the school. The difficulties become apparent in the more interactive strands, and we may find we have painted ourselves into a corner. As an example, it may be stated categorically (usually in response to teacher pressure) that a student who swears at a member of staff is automatically suspended, absolutely cut and dried. In reality, what quite often happens is that when a senior member of staff is teasing out such an encounter, they may discover what they feel are extenuating circumstances for the student's loss of control. They may be faced with a distressed and contrite youngster and may then be reluctant, or even refuse to suspend. The failure to suspend a pupil may prove very damaging to the morale of the larger group of staff which takes the more empirical view, i.e. swearing equals suspension. Therein lies one of the inherent difficulties of a discipline policy that relies too heavily on the hierarchical approach. The person dealing with the offending youngster may well be the next person up the line as per the policy, but that person may have no emotional stake in the situation. This may be very useful at times it must be said, in order to shine the cold light of dispassionate logic, but unlikely to satisfy the teacher who has been pushed firmly into 'reptilian' mode by the stress of the encounter.

Hard and soft issues

It is our contention, therefore, that a discipline policy should be composed of two strands – the so-called 'hard' issues which encompass everything that can be negotiated with all stakeholders and cannot be muddied by the effects of pupil–teacher or parent–teacher interactions. The other, 'soft', issues could be classified as a behaviour management plan, and as such should be included in the school's development document, and should answer the question 'How do we want it to be?' If we can clarify our expectation in the context of our own institution, we can then perhaps use the behaviour management plan to answer the second question 'How are we going to get there?'

The behavioural culture

Research into behavioural issues tends to look for influences in four distinct areas – the neighbourhood, the institution, the classroom, the student – which we would describe as an ecosystem.

All the major processes of this ecosystem have an effect on behaviour within it, the behaviour of staff, students and parents alike. Decisions taken in any of the four areas will have behavioural implications, and the behaviour management plan must acknowledge this and indicate ways in which we are aware of behavioural costs, and have strategies to minimise them.

To dwell on a single influence can be a sterile process and at worst a futile one. Effective action begins with the recognition of the contingent effect of those areas of influence and continues with the pragmatic and optimistic search for solutions within all these areas. This has implications for communication, since ignorance of the purpose of any measure can and will breed mistrust. This applies to teachers, students and parents.

We cannot afford to be imprecise or vague. If, for example, we want all our students to wear a school uniform, we must state precisely why, and what useful effects we believe that enforcing the wearing of a uniform brings. We must also be aware of the behavioural cost that the wearing of a uniform may bring and present strategies to overcome this. Furthermore, we have to share this with all our stakeholders – constantly. Progress is not always readily identifiable or quantifiable, and this is in the nature of our dealings with the emotional brain – no 'quick fixes' here, rather the long haul and the constant and ever-present struggle for solutions.

The search for solutions is made easier if we notionally, and for practical purposes, separate these areas. We can then identify threats to good order within each element before putting the behavioural development plan together into a coherent and more effective whole, without losing sight of the fact that we are dealing with people's emotional brains. The nature of the solutions must take this into account. Of the four major influences on behavioural issues let us firstly, consider the neighbourhood in more detail.

Engaging the neighbourhood

If the neighbourhood of the school provides a threat to good order, we may decide to try to minimise that threat by bringing the neighbourhood into the school, allowing community use of the school's facilities, for example . . .

- Organise events for pupils and their parents that are rewarding and unthreatening – school shows, OAP parties, celebrations of achievement, etc.
- Providing a welcoming entrance – signs saying welcome (in many languages if you are in a multi-ethnic area)
- Posters for non-readers that provide the same message
- A supermarket style photograph board showing pictures of staff who can help
- A carefully planned programme of enrichment for the pupils.

The support of parents is an absolutely invaluable aid to good relations between teachers and pupils. The fostering of these relations is a vital part of the synergy that can be created by mutual trust and shared aspirations. How difficult a task this can be however, clouded as it often is by the emotional responses of both parties in any encounter. A school's behavioural plan may enumerate all those occasions on which a parent may interact with teachers and management, but it must also indicate strategies to facilitate those occasions where the parent is a reluctant participant. Controlled and planned meetings with parents present less of a challenge than the impromptu ones.

For many parents there is a tension between school and home (there are too many reasons to develop here). Broadly speaking, parents may seek to defend their children, as the emotional brain dictates, often in situations where they discover that they are quite probably indefensible. They will seek to minimise the difficulties, or to justify their children's responses to a given situation. Teachers are frequently disappointed by a seeming lack of support from parents. Naïve, perhaps, given what we know about the emotional response.

The keynotes in dealing with parents, certainly with reasonable parents, are a sharing of purpose, a sharing of the mutual regard for the rights of their child, and a sharing of the day-to-day struggle that both parent and teacher may be involved in. The first encounter with a parent is likely to be the crucial one, if the teacher remains calm and purposeful it should set the agenda for future meetings. It would be naïve and unhelpful to suggest that all our dealings with parents are likely to be trouble-free. Many parents do not avail themselves of the opportunity to meet their child's teachers through the usual channels. Parent's evenings generally do not provide an opportunity for the parents of our difficult youngsters. For these parents, for whom the school is a hostile place, often based on their own experiences, extra efforts to engage their emotional brains will be necessary.

Many people hate hospitals, they only need to smell the inside of the building to feel high levels of anxiety and fear based on previous experience or perceptions. Those working in the hospital building on a daily basis find it difficult to accept the level of fear their workplace engenders. The same is true of schools. There are many adults, now parents, who have unpleasant, fearful memories or perceptions of schools as organisations and teachers as people. These anxieties and fears can have dramatic effects on an individual's approach to any involvement with school culture. So, as adults returning to school to support or defend our children, our feelings will be influenced significantly by our early education experiences. Where these emotions are particularly strong, the behavioural effects on entering the school will be evident. This is then overlaid with the emotions which derive from their present reason for their visit, which may contain highly charged emotional responses. This is not the ideal emotional state to discuss a pupil's challenging behaviour and possible need for parental involvement in the target setting process.

We can call on outside agencies to help us, social work, community education, for example, but aggressive, hostile and unreasonable parents are an ever-present for many of us. We are all aware that the parent who bursts over the threshold in full reptilian mode, demanding their rights and demanding to see 'somebody' can present a real challenge. Like their children, however, if faced with implacable calm and cool professionalism, they will not reduce us to responding in kind. This, at least, leaves open the possibility of improving any conflict in the future, and above all, leaves us feeling that we have dealt with a difficult situation with some skill.

Sometimes we deal with parents who are so volatile, and even dangerous, that we may decide that dealings with these parents need to be conducted in situations where a teacher is never unsupported.

The second of the four major influences we will consider is that of the students themselves. At this stage we are looking at communicating with the student body en masse. We will focus on the individual in subsequent chapters.

SORRY – I'M ONLY THE CARETAKER

Engaging the pupil culture

By considering the already established events and special occasions in the school calendar it is possible to develop a coherence in the messages communicated through the events. For example, a carefully planned programme of enrichment for the pupils, delivered through selected year group assemblies, could include

- visits from educational drama groups
- musicians
- local role models
- multicultural awareness raising
- social skills and citizenship
- health professionals
- healthy eating competitions.

The success of such events will be characterised by effective pre-planning and vigorous 'stage management' – careful logistics, deployment of staff and having a plan B! And . . . having a plan C!

Third, the influence of the institution is obviously major, but is possibly one of the most difficult to view objectively from 'inside'. We very quickly lose the first-impressions view of the school and feel comfortable with the familiar whether we agree with it or not. It is important to examine ways in which the 'visitors' view can be used to develop and improve the school.

Engaging the institution

Institutional factors are often those over which teachers feel that they have least control:

- the nature of the building
- unsympathetic time-tabling
- the size of teaching group
- lack of resources/unfair distribution of resources
- the demands created by external pressures
- nationally assessed courses
- inclusion
- the calibre of the students

This is by no means an exhaustive list! It may be important to lessen the sense of impotence teachers may experience by such factors as these.

To prevent such matters being only in the remit of the senior management team, and to create a wider sense of empowerment, it may be sensible to create a forum within the institution where such issues can be aired and if possible addressed. A forum should be constituted in such a way as to have the will to recommend, and the power to implement, any changes in response to an identified need. It must be accessible and 'user-friendly' and enjoy the trust of everyone. Above all, it must be pro-active, i.e. anticipate problems and seek pre-emptive solutions. It is important that all staff feel that they have a voice regardless of their position in the school's hierarchy, and a behaviour forum can provide that voice. The forum should be representative of all and its membership should reflect that, with a balance of genders, of young and inexperienced, along with seasoned campaigners. A blend of hawks and doves is desirable also, but will need careful handling. The forum should be chaired by a member of the senior management team – this will provide the potency.

It is also important that everyone who serves on this group is a volunteer and not a conscript. It's useful to change the membership from time to time to prevent staleness and to renew optimism. At one school I know, this forum has evolved and become a Rewards Group, whose function primarily is to address staff concerns by exploring rewards and incentives to minimise poor behaviour. Pupils and parents have a voice too, and there should be a mechanism for allowing representation from them. The deliberations of this forum should be considered, and where appropriate should be embedded in the behaviour plan as part of its ongoing and organic development.

Given a normal distribution amongst staff of positive and optimistic people against negative and cynical ones, such an approach can go some way to engaging the 'critical mass', provided the search for solutions is characterised by a 'no blame' and pragmatic approach.

The behaviour forum could have a role to play in evaluating and pointing up the successful aspects of the behaviour plan – since we have a tendency to lose sight of our successes in the midst of trying to cope with seemingly ever-present or new difficulties. Reminding ourselves of when we have been successful increases our sense of being in control and provides us with the emotional wherewithal for the next challenge. Teasing out the successful elements can give insights into just how we should approach presenting difficulties. A forum of this nature can simply be a group of staff focussing on an area of concern and seeking solutions as a group. The forum should be constantly seeking for rewards and incentives to enhance the message of the behaviour plan.

Having seen groups function very successfully, we can commend such a forum to all schools, but particularly to those schools where poor behaviour is a very real issue.

3 The Big Picture

Behavioural patterns in the academic year

Having considered the human perspective of the emotional brain and its effect on interaction and behaviour we then moved to the major influences of the neighbourhood, the institution and the pupils. From the teachers' perspective these often feel like the things we have to accept. Being able to identify and view these influences objectively gives us the opportunity to optimise the effect of our collective actions. We can though have most influence on the environment within our own classrooms, with the pupils we teach. As we have seen behaviour is not a simplistic issue and we must have some awareness of the context in which we are operating.

We must begin with the big picture, the overview, in order to clarify our own thinking about where we want to go. In the process we will also construct a means to provide feedback for ourselves and our pupils about the progress we have made. We know from experience that the academic year has several predictable patterns, by defining these patterns we gain information about behaviour. We can use the information to inform our understanding of the behaviours and to identify strategies which will be useful in our responses.

Bill Rogers identifies two phases of the academic year, the establishment and consolidation phases. We would also identify the transition phase. For each of these phases there are typical behaviours for both adults and pupils. We should also seek those particular characteristics of our own school context which leads to predictable behaviours. We need to look at our academic calendar and plot significant behavioural issues. We have constructed a sample behaviour calendar in chapter 4 for clarity, but these influences are by no means exhaustive. We can include anything which we feel may have a significant influence on either pupil or adult behaviour. We can then use this knowledge of the academic year in our school to help us pace the behavioural learning. This in turn will enable us to be realistic about our behavioural expectations of our pupils and ourselves.

Establishing the behaviour action plan

The behaviour action plan will have distinct phases. The establishment phase must contain all the elements previously discussed to set parameters and address the expectations of all stakeholders.

In term 1 two major themes need to be addressed,

1   How do we want it to be?
2   How are we going to get there?

The beginning of a new school year is characterised by high energy on the part of the staff, and as such, presents the optimum time to establish consensus and mobilise broad support. Managing behaviour is important for all schools naturally, but for those of us working in what could be called challenging areas, it becomes the major priority. Raising attainment in schools like these depends very much on our being able to minimise pupil disruption. Significant in-service time needs to be devoted to this – to re-affirm objectives with experienced staff and to provide a useful and structured induction to new and inexperienced ones.

The first day of term, the 'teachers only' day, must be used, in part at least, to detail the discipline policy and behaviour action plan for the term ahead, and to re-visit the school's positive behaviour management strategies. It could take the form of a single sheet of A4 giving brief details of the school's behavioural plan over, say, the next 6 weeks. It certainly should not be a 'tome' but must flag up the behavioural priorities and the strategies intended to reinforce those priorities. It is most important for the school's management team to foster optimism at this time by stating their intentions of providing support and encouragement, and then hopefully being seen to do so. The beginning of the school year is also the time when our students are at their most receptive, and so it is imperative that we seek to establish the behaviours that we want during this time, in our classrooms in particular, and around the school in general. Assemblies during this time will reflect this and will deal broadly with sharing the school rules and the expectations of good behaviour in social areas and corridors. We can drive home the message with posters and signs around the school, drawing pupils' attention to them constantly.

A strong staff presence at change of lessons, intervals and lunch times will moderate poor behaviour. We can introduce the likelihood of incentives and rewards at this stage for our pupils to aspire to:

- Class of the month
- Litter busters award
- Reward disco
- Uniform spot checks – tuck shop vouchers to everyone in the class in full uniform
- Good news letters home
- Genuine warmth and approval
- Attendance and punctuality challenges
- Reward assemblies for academic and behavioural achievement
- School photographic, certificate displays of specific behavioural achievement
- Opportunity to earn reward activities.

These rewards should not be too long in coming, in order to reinforce the message and to keep the momentum going. This is particularly important for our S1/Year 7 students, given that early intervention is known to minimise the difficulties that may present later on.

These measures are likely to be sufficient for the greater number of our students, but it is likely that there will be a significant minority for whom more will be needed. The earlier we are able to identify such needs the more effective our intervention is likely to be.

An early warning system

In order to target appropriate support as early as possible, it is important to liaise with previous teachers as fully as time allows before our pupils enter our doors. Such liaison can identify those pupils for whom any transition is likely to be a struggle – for whatever reasons. The information could identify candidates for a summer school, for example, or those who will need an early programme to enhance their social skills. An intensive monitoring of these pupils over a finite period by all teaching staff will provide much useful information to the school's support for learning staff. This would include being as well informed as possible about the youngsters in front of them, since ignorance reduces empowerment. This must be done in the spirit of giving all youngsters a fresh start, naturally. Whilst we may all in discussion agree that this fresh start approach is essential, the day-to-day demands of putting it into practice often feel very different.

The effect of teacher behaviour

By accepting the influential role of teacher, we must take responsibility for the effects of our own behaviour on the teaching and learning interaction. Research indicates that 85% of communication is non-verbal. It is obviously in our best interests therefore to examine our own communication skills to raise awareness of the messages we give. Body language and facial expressions can be subtle vehicles for communication. As adults we often misinterpret such communication from others. If it is true that as adults we are still learning and practising these skills, then it is also true that our pupils have had even less opportunity to practise. In order to be clear about the messages we are giving and to make them as effective as possible we need to make sure that our, tone of voice, body stance, facial expression and language are all working congruently. The way in which we move around the classroom, towards and away from pupils, all give messages about the emotions we are experiencing. Pupils will draw conclusions from their interpretations of our non-verbal communication.

The same applies to every social interaction. General messages will be collected for students to build knowledge of us as people and as a basis for predicting our reactions to particular situations. These perceptions will be continually adapted in the light of their experience of us. Needless to say, while this is going on we are doing the same to those around us.

As teachers, it is important that we believe that behaviour can change. Every behaviour has an effect, if we stand very close to someone they will interpret this action and either encourage us to move closer or encourage us to move away. Smiling a greeting will generally evoke a smile in return; allowing someone into the traffic queue in front of us will encourage the driver to do the same for someone else. We can use this knowledge to positively affect classroom behaviour. By consciously using verbal and non-verbal communication in complementary ways, we can optimise the effectiveness of our communication.

We have identified four assumptions which underpin positive behaviour management:

1   The behaviour of teachers influences the behaviour of pupils.
2   Techniques of classroom management can be identified and learned.
3   Teachers must take responsibility for developing their skill.
4   Effective teachers are skilled at minimising problems.

The in-sets in this book provide a journey to the consensus described in these assumptions, and is a very important part of changing our practice. Discussions can and do lead to the belief that we are not impotent in the face of increasing pupil disruption, rather we can, in a supportive environment, seek solutions, try them out, refine them and regain a measure of control.

We must consider in some detail how we would like our classroom community to run and some of the influences that will affect the dynamics of the real situation. As we have previously stated, the teacher will be the major influence in the development of relationships in this community. Every member of the community will be learning. The whole focus of the community needs to be learning in its widest sense.

To be most effective in teaching we must bring our personal learning to a conscious level. Learning can be a curious activity. For example, we often experience anxiety about new learning because we feel we should already know what we are being taught. This may sound illogical, but most learning anxiety is centred on the approach to, or initial stages of activities. To view ourselves as learners within the class community enables us to share experiences with pupils from a different perspective. Our learning may not be curriculum-based, but it will be related to learning about the individuals, their behaviour and relationships in the class community. The person we learn most about will probably be ourselves. Being able to reflect on our own responses and reactions will enable us to identify more accurately the most effective ways to manage our own behaviour. In the same way, we will be better informed to support pupils to do the same.

We can view the task of managing a classroom as having two specific strands, managing the setting and managing the demands generated by the classroom situation. The result of effective classroom management is that it involves and unites members of the class community.

Managing the setting	*Managing the demands generated by the classroom situation*
Resources	Sharing expectations
Seating arrangements	Being vigilant and aware
Teaching style	Purposeful in demeanour
Preparedness	Personable in style
Ensure an orderly start/dismissal	Being authoritative

Research indicates that the approving, optimistic, helpful and consistently firm teacher is the preferred model for pupils. We are continually making adjustments to our personal teaching approach in response to the situations in which we find ourselves. From the table, the elements of the left column need to be in place to facilitate those in the right column. Neither list is exhaustive but can be used to guide our developing effective personal teaching style. In the same way that our awareness of our own behavioural responses continue to develop in a social context, our responses in the school context will do the same.

4 Consensus-driven behaviour planning within the classroom

Although we can be clear about what we wish to include in the behaviour action plan in our classroom, we need to relate it to whole school principles to increase its effectiveness. Working in isolation within a school is not only very lonely and difficult, but it also minimises the effectiveness of our work. Finding ways to make the whole school principles a reality in your classroom opens up opportunities to explore the common currency with colleagues and increase consistency.

Equally, the pupils need to be involved in the establishment and development of the behaviour plan. The greater involvement the pupils have at this stage, the easier it will be to encourage individual awareness and responsibility for personal and group behaviour. Pupils can discuss and agree the principles of the community rules as well as formulating the actual wording. Taking this discussion a stage further it is possible to examine with pupils, the observable behaviours which will evidence the agreed rules. We can then clarify and teach the appropriate expectations. Using photographic displays with pupil interpretation and personalisation of the rules provides a useful reference point to support the implementation of the rules.

Relating rules to rewards and consequences through class and group discussion provides a common understanding and behaviour framework within which all agree to work. It is essential that teachers include themselves in this process and give examples of maintaining their own behaviour according to the agreed rules. As adults in school, we must be seen to model appropriate behaviour. Rewards and consequences for behaviour can generate some very positive and enlightening discussion. It is possible to develop this idea to include pupil and teacher contracts which clarify expectations of each party.

During the establishment phase, it will be necessary to prove that the behaviour action plan is a reality. This can be done by:

- frequently referring to the display
- involving pupils in resolving issues where appropriate
- evidencing consistent application of the rules.

The effect of this type of framework is to increase the predictability of responses, and therefore the security of those in the class community. It is then easier to build a personal script based on the agreed rewards and consequences which fit the framework.

Increasingly, curriculum pressures are making teachers feel that they should not spend time on such activities. We believe however, that we cannot afford to neglect the effective teaching of behaviour. We believe that if the will is there the behavioural curriculum can be successfully taught through every curriculum area.

The sample behaviour calendar shows how certain predictable elements of the academic year play their part in influencing the behaviour of ourselves and our pupils. Each teacher could add their own personal influences both positive and negative.

We can include a variety of events and acknowledge a variety of emotions on our personal behaviour calendar. For example, being aware that we find the beginnings of term an anxious time, or that energy levels are particularly low in January and February. The next step is to match typical behaviours around the items included on the calendar. For example, considering the three phases of the year, establishment, consolidation and transition, we can begin to identify certain predictable pupil behaviours.

The establishment phase is a time when the foundations of relationships are formed or reformed. It involves finding our individual place in the school and class community in relation to others. This is true of adults and pupils! We are all subject to the following behavioural issues:

- challenging boundaries
- testing the consistency of your responses
- trying to manipulate the adults
- anxieties about coping with new routines
- finding where our place is in the hierarchy
- opportunity for a fresh start
- checking out preconceived ideas of each other
- anxieties about work levels
- resistance to work tasks through anxiety
- feeling unsure of previous learning
- lack of confidence in approaching new learning.

The consolidation phase is in some ways a more comfortable phase of the year. We all know each other a little better, we can predict the behavioural responses of those around us. The downside is that we may feel that it is not possible to change the less positive responses. The typical behavioural issues will include:

- feeling generally more confident
- responses more predictable
- relationships established
- predictable responses to work tasks
- routines established and generally accepted
- individual progress within predictable limits

- rules, rights and responsibilities established
- rules actively used to maintain classroom ethos
- predictable responses between significant personalities
- patterns of behaviour accepted as unchangeable.

The transition phase often feels like a shock to the system, just when you thought it was safe . . .! The anxiety levels rise because everyone is aware of the impending changes. The emotions are a mixture of excitement, fear and vulnerability, they affect both pupils and adults. So, the predictable behavioural responses will include:

- general anxiety and unsettled atmosphere in class
- predictable ways of provoking conflict situations
- relationships strained
- anxiety about next placement
- returning to previous difficult behaviours to prove not ready to move on
- using previous behaviours to express fear of change.

Having identified these behaviour patterns the issue is to use this knowledge to prepare ourselves and to maximise the opportunity for behavioural learning. There would be no point for example, in expecting the bulk of conceptually new learning to take place at the end of the Summer term. The part which behaviour plays in the academic year is talked about anecdotally in staffrooms extensively but we are seldom in a position to step back, look at the wider picture and use the knowledge to advantage. Teachers' skill in facilitating pupil learning is awe inspiring when there is consideration of all the factors involved. The next chapter examines the opportunity of harnessing this skill and applying it to behavioural issues.

Month	September	October	November	December
Phase	*Establishment*	*Establishment*	*Establishment*	*Establishment*
Behaviour influences	New class New relationships New routines Trying out consistency of response	Half term holiday Changes in weather and season	Onset of Winter Wet and windy weather, wet playtimes Parents evenings School fair	Christmas School productions and events
Personal issues	Feelings of starting again Having to establish desired routines and systems	Frustration, routines and behaviour management still being established	Tiredness levels increasing Too much to do, not enough time before Christmas	Particular pressure on managing work and home demands

Month	January	February	March	April
Phase	*Consolidation*	*Consolidation*	*Consolidation*	*Consolidation*
Behaviour influences	Relationships established for better or worse! Responses between adults and pupils predictable, for better or worse!	More wet playtimes Snow Covering for absent colleagues Parents evenings	Clocks change signalling longer days	End of term Warmer brighter weather but still some wet days School journey
Personal issues	Pressure for evidence of pupil progress Anxiety and frustration about individual pupil behavioural response	Want to spend time involved in personal interests	Dissatisfaction, thoughts of applying for new job	End of term tiredness and pressure to complete record keeping

Month	May	June	July	August
Phase	*Transition*	*Transition*	*Transition*	*Recuperation*
Behaviour influences	Standard tests Exams	Preparing to move to next class/year group/school	Reports Records of achievement	Domestic demands replace work demands
Personal issues	Frustration and anxiety	Concern about which class(es) we will be teaching next Comparison of achievement between last year and this year, between classes Is it them or me?	Helplessness, did pupils achieve as much as they could, what will I do differently next year What will their next teacher think of their progress?	Prepare for starting again Tiredness, anxiety, excitement

5 Behaviour – taught not caught, making the message clear

When first meeting a class previously taught by colleagues, we are aware of particular names and characters for a variety of reasons. We are also under a certain pressure, depending on our relationship with the colleague, to corroborate or contradict their views. By going through the process of considering our own, and the pupils' responses to the establishment phase we introduce an element of detachment, which allows a different view of the situation. This subtle change then enhances the opportunity for the new beginning being used as an opportunity for change. The alternative is for us all to be trapped into fulfilling the stereotypes already in place.

Teachers are extremely skilled in planning, amending, differentiating and delivering the curriculum. If we are able to view behaviour in the same framework, we can support pupils to learn relationship and life skills, which they may have no other opportunity to learn. Drawing the parallel between curriculum and behaviour is a useful tool in maintaining perspective on progress and realistic expectations. We do not expect pupils in a reception class to complete calculus activities but we do expect them to be able to exhibit levels of self-control and conformity, which may be completely alien to their experience and understanding.

Many behaviours and significant elements of language are peculiar to school contexts. For example where else would a child be asked, 'Are you a hot dinner?' Many classrooms have language which is not common to the rest of the school. For example, finished trays, zebra group, brave writing. Communication and language are fundamental to the behavioural curriculum, unless we are explicit about our meaning and seek clarification of others' understanding we will be doomed to a context of confusing mixed messages. Our contention would be that in many schools that could be a good description of the present situation.

Returning to the theme of congruence, having drafted our behaviour plan it is useful to draw out key messages which we wish to convey about how things work in our classroom or school. For example, making mistakes is an opportunity to learn, we listen to each other, honesty is valued. The next task is to consider how we can consistently reiterate these key messages. This is particularly true of the establishment phase as the foundations for class community life are put in place. Obviously, there is no point in valuing the idea of making mistakes as an opportunity to learn if our response in the daily situation is to get angry and remonstrate with the pupil concerned.

ASKING FOR TROUBLE?

We have so far considered mainly our own classroom context. In constructing our behavioural view of our class community, we cannot ignore the whole school context. No classroom is an island, nor does it function in a vacuum. Ideally the classroom priorities should exemplify those of the whole school. In this situation, there is the greatest opportunity for pupils to learn consistently about the effects of positive behaviour management in a microcosm of society. Although life is seldom ideal, we should be able to find within the broad aims or mission statement of the school, an opportunity for developing a teaching approach to positive behaviour management. Our personal influence on behavioural approaches within the school will be dependent on our place within the hierarchy and our effective sphere of influence. The establishment phase of the year is a time when there is most opportunity for change, in the same way that it is for the pupils in our classes. This may be an unsettling or an exciting prospect for individuals, which will affect their ability to maximise the opportunity, but it will be a reality.

We can use the priorities we have already identified to consider how we relate to other classes and communities within the school. If we work from how we would like it to be, then we can look for school systems which provide opportunity for us to build towards our goals. One of the key issues will be the currency of the relationship between classes; it may be competitive, supportive, positive or negative. Whatever it is at present there is always opportunity for positive change. We can develop supportive professional relationships with colleagues through planning groups, initiating positive discussions about behaviour, negotiating mutually supportive arrangements for behavioural issues, co-colleague moderation of academic and behavioural expectations.

Opening such communication links enhances the possibility of greater consistency of response to behaviour, whilst developing a supportive network to increase individual confidence and secure decision-making.

One of the implications of considering behaviour as an area of the curriculum, is that we are able to identify a baseline of competence and the next learning steps. We then need to identify the support required to achieve the new learning. In some cases, this will be teaching and the opportunity to focus on and practice new skills for a whole class. For example, particularly in the establishment phase you may decide to focus on entering and leaving the room in an acceptable manner for a specific number of days. As with all learning some pupils will grasp the concept immediately, others will need further teaching, encouragement and support.

Managing adults in the classroom

The teacher in the classroom manages those present in the classroom. This will happen whether we do it consciously or not. The result is that where we leave the management to chance, an opportunity to communicate our key principles has been lost or at best diluted. On the other hand, we can use the way we relate to others as a key opportunity to role model ways of interacting and negotiating.

A major difficulty of working with other adults in the classroom is trying to make time to share planning or information. However, clearly setting out what we see as the key factors in our management of the classroom can help to ensure that we are working towards the same goals. To minimise opportunity for misunderstanding, it is always useful to clarify expectations of the role each adult will play, including ourselves. By being explicit about our behavioural objectives and the need for every opportunity to model appropriate interactions to be maximised we can have a powerful foundation from which pupils can learn. An essential factor will be that our interactions with both adults and pupils must follow the same principles.

These principles must also be congruent with the policy of the school. For example, we are aware that to provide the optimum conditions for learning pupils need to feel emotionally and physically safe. This can be achieved through consistency of response and reaction to situations. Building a class community in which pupils are able to take risks in their learning with appropriate support takes time, but begins with our entrance into the room. The way in which we welcome others to the learning session confirms first impressions of how we will respond. By relating new learning to previous experience we can encourage confidence and reduce the risk factor for some pupils.

The more detail in which the behavioural influence of adults can be agreed, the more effective the impact. Having agreed the key principles we want to communicate, our own responses need to be considered in terms of the more subtle messages they carry. This can be done individually on reflection, but is more effective if reflection is with a colleague, ideally one who has shared the experience.

Any management situation is about achieving a constructive balance between control and empowerment. The essence of a good manager is one who can find the right balance for the right people in the right situation. The identification of management as a skill within the teacher's armoury is essential in considering behaviour in the classroom. Behaviour is always a management issue, getting the detail right can make the difference between an escalation of inappropriate behaviour or a return to the expectations of the classroom.

6   Managing the emotional environment in the classroom

Having identified the predictable presenting behaviours for the establishment phase of the academic year we can begin to make conscious decisions about how to manage them. It is important to remember that the same responses are evident in adults as well as the pupils. Equally there may be others not listed which are significant for us personally, for example some of us generally find beginnings exciting and stimulating, but endings difficult and stressful. By identifying our personal feelings about the different stages of the year we can also begin to manage our own behaviour and be aware of the effect it will have on our perception of events.

To develop effective behaviour management strategies for ourselves we need to be able to accurately identify our emotions at any given point in time. To enhance this process it is useful to reflect on the very first sign that we are feeling anxious, angry, frightened etc. By doing this we are able to buy some time to employ management strategies appropriate to the specific context. This may be taking a deep breath and walking away or verbally signalling our feelings to those involved before the situation escalates. Once the emotion is effective beyond our first indicators we are less able to control our responses. Logically then, highly charged emotional situations are not a time to begin employing behaviour management strategies.

Having acknowledged our own emotional responses and predicted the presenting behaviours of our pupils for the first stage of the academic year, we are able to take this as a baseline for constructing a behaviour plan for the establishment phase.

The classroom community

Our class is in effect a community, a transient but a functioning community all the same. Each member of the community will establish a place in the community and have a role to play. We must also clarify, individually, what we see as the role of teacher and learners in our own context. For effective use of appropriate behaviour management strategies there must be congruency of philosophy between what we are trying to achieve and the way in which we try to achieve it. There would be no point in employing strategies, which give opportunity for experimental behavioural learning on behalf of pupils if we require high levels of situational control as teachers. Although it would be an onerous task to detail all the factors which make up our teaching style, it is possible to broadly describe our preferred teacher role. For example, facilitator, dictator, learning partner, learning manager etc. It is useful to then clarify our view of the role of the pupil and be aware of a congruent approach. If we see ourselves as facilitators, it would be difficult to succeed if we expect pupils to be seen and not heard.

Levels of control

Clearly, there is a need for the adults in a school to exert a level of control in the classroom context. However, defining this level of control would be a complex process and of questionable value. What is evident, is that teachers, as individuals, require different levels of control to facilitate effective teaching situations. Before considering a behaviour plan, it is useful to identify what would indicate to us that we have a sufficiently controlled situation. Listing the factors, which would indicate to us that the situation was under- or over-controlled enables us to find the comfort zone in which we feel able to teach most effectively. Obviously the levels of control will be affected by a variety of factors, such as the physical environment, i.e. classroom, hall, field and the type of lesson. Raising our awareness of what we are willing and able to tolerate helps us to take effective preventative action at the first sign of boundaries being stretched. The alternative is 'firefighting', when things have escalated and emotions are having a greater influence on everyone's behaviour.

The establishment phase of the year is characteristically a time for laying the foundations for the systems and relationships which will develop within our classroom community for the duration of the academic year. It is important to emphasise that this will happen whether we plan for it or leave it to chance. Everyone who spends time in our classroom will learn about behaviour. They will learn how to gain attention, influence decisions, be listened to, maintain their place in the social hierarchy etc. We have a choice, leave it to chance or teach social and emotional literacy through a reality-based situation. Initially this may feel like 'something else' we need to do, but in reality, it is an investment in prevention, which will minimise the amount of time needed to deal with inappropriate behaviour.

Identifying realistic behavioural expectations

By drafting out our behavioural expectations for each phase of the year, we are also able to gain feedback to monitor real progress rather than be deluded into believing that things are either better or worse than the reality. It is important to maintain some view of our priorities. Identify what is essential for pupils to know and practise to participate effectively in our classroom community. This needs to be balanced with what is essential for us to know and practise in our classroom community. Our knowledge of our pupils builds minute by minute over the year, we could write a significant volume about each individual without any further research, particularly about their behaviour. We miss a valuable opportunity if we do not use this knowledge to inform the learning of our pupils.

The teacher–pupil relationship

> Events in the classroom are influenced by a complex equation of expectations, attitudes, policies and laws which are shaped by forces at work in the classroom, the school, the local community and by society as a whole.
>
> Elton Report (DES and Welsh Office, 1989)

There can be no denial that the classroom is at the heart of all these influences and central to the classroom is the relationship between teacher and pupil. The key assumption that we must make then is that our behaviour as teachers is the biggest influence on the behaviour of our pupils. This requires us to be scrupulous in the management of our own behaviour first and foremost.

If we accept that behaviour is everything we do and everything we say, then we also accept that as the central influence in the classroom our behaviour must model everything we want from our pupils in terms of their behaviour. This is particularly important in the early encounters with a class. We must establish what we want from our pupils by demonstrating this very clearly with our own behaviour towards them. We also need to be clear in our own minds just what we do require from our pupils, so that we can make it clear to them by all the processes available to us in the classroom.

There is no point in putting up a sign 'You are now entering a positive language zone', if the first words a pupil hears from us are negative ones.

By discussion and negotiation with our pupils, we can frame behaviours that we jointly consider to be appropriate for our classroom. 'Our' in this case implying pupils and teacher in partnership. By modelling that behaviour we give ourselves a powerful lever. We can safely remind a pupil about any of our agreed rules. For example, 'That's inappropriate, William. You know the rule about . . .'.

This should be said without heat in the first instance, placing the responsibility squarely on the pupil for breaking an agreed covenant. Safe in the knowledge also that the pupil is unable to return the reprimand with accusations about our behaviour as the teacher. The use of the word 'inappropriate' is quite important since it implies that the pupil knows what is appropriate, to themselves, the class and the teacher.

Careful use of reprimand can go a long way towards restoring peace in the classroom and lowering the emotional stakes in any encounter. 'Watch your tone, Sarah' is less likely to bring a combative response than 'Don't speak to me in that tone' even if the latter is what our emotional brain is telling us to say.

If we accept that learning and teaching are the central purposes of the classroom it becomes vital to deal with disruption in the least costly and least intrusive way. Our goals are to minimise the loss of momentum, to avoid escalation and to return to a task as quickly as possible. In no way does this represent a soft option for our pupils, nor does it represent capitulation on the part of the teacher. Using the knowledge that we have about the way the human brain functions we can now be quite certain that no learning can take place if, by our own behaviour, we contribute to a 'reptilian' response in our pupils. Furthermore, by entering into a confrontation with a pupil we are ensuring that none of the other pupils in the class will stay on task since more entertainment is likely to be provided by the drama unfolding before their eyes.

It's ridiculous to suggest that we can always avoid confrontation, many pupils will deliberately try to provoke us to and we will always be stressed by such encounters. As long as the provocation has come from the pupil and we have not responded in kind then we will have done as much as we should.

Reducing disruption is a realistic aim, eliminating it is an impossible dream.

It is useless to ask questions such as:

- Why do 2 year olds have tantrums?
- Why do adolescents always have to challenge authority?
- Why do young people behave differently when they are in a group?

The answer is – because they do! Which of course is no answer at all. However, being aware of this should result in our being prepared for that disruption when it occurs, as it inevitably will.

Having a thorough knowledge of the age and stage of our pupils will give us insight into what is appropriate to expect from them. We are well aware of this as parents, but seem less sure as teachers. Each age group presents its own challenges.

Preparing for the establishment phase

Using the behaviour plan, previously described, we can identify our own list of how we will lay the foundations for the effective class community. Developing the list to include how we will communicate the elements is what will help to make it a reality. For example,

Establishment phase: a personal plan – sample

1   Personal behavioural boundaries and priorities detailed. For example, everyone must ask if they wish to leave the room during a lesson, anyone wishing to speak must indicate by raising their hand, noise levels will be agreed according to activity taking place, difficulties with work tasks can be communicated to adults in a variety of agreed ways.

2   Five positively phrased class rules discussed and negotiated with all involved. For example:

- in our class we will listen to each other
- in our class we will support our own and others' learning through our appropriate behaviour
- in our class we will put equipment away when we have finished
- in our class when we move around the room we will do so quietly and carefully
- in our class we will talk through problems when we feel angry.

The wording of the rules will be dependent on the age and stage of the pupils. Once the rules have been agreed, useful discussion can take place about what members of the class community will be doing in specific situations if they are within the rules.

3   Reward systems and consequences are negotiated and agreed in a graduated list matched with examples of behaviours. These can also be related directly to the agreed class rules as well as taking account of the whole school systems.

4   The currency of the class will be positive. This will be communicated by using specific praise to highlight appropriate behaviour and cue others to mirror that behaviour, in order to receive positive attention.

5   Every behavioural situation will be used to teach appropriate behaviour and communicate clear expectations.

6   Consistency will be monitored through discussion with all involved in the classroom community and evidenced through use of rewards and sanctions.

7   Communication links with home situations will involve both academic and behavioural achievement. Information will be provided at the earliest opportunity of difficulties being experienced and strategies to be employed to support. Monitoring and review of progress will be a three-way process involving, the pupil, adults from home and adults from school.

7 Managing the physical environment in the classroom

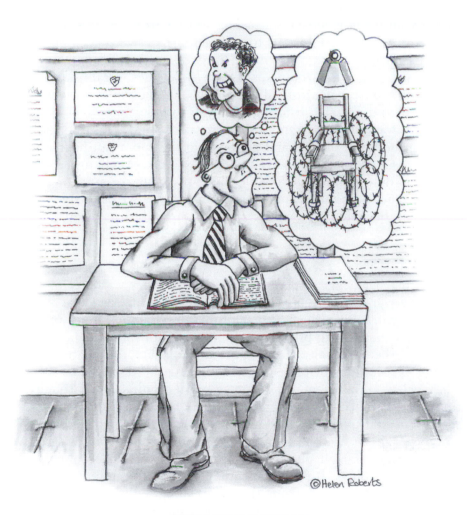

PREPARING THE GROUND

Many education textbooks talk about organising the classroom, thinking about the placing of resources and pupils. There is a significant difference in considering the classroom environment from a behavioural viewpoint; we begin to see the room from the pupils' point of view. We will not be able to control all the physical aspects of the classroom but we can make the best of the influence we can exert. As with other means of communication if we consciously decide on the messages we wish to give, we can ensure that the message is consistent through as many routes as possible. This will make the message more powerful and effective.

The physical environment around us can significantly affect the way we feel; needless to say this is true of our pupils as well. There is naturally a connection between how we feel and how we behave. By making conscious decisions about the displays and arrangements of furniture we can influence the atmosphere of the classroom. We can give messages about the purpose of the room, enhancing the elements, which communicate the need for working together, and developing the opportunity available for pupils to influence the physical environment. This could be through being involved in deciding seating arrangements or displays of work, for example. It is important to differentiate between making the room look attractive and using the environment to reinforce and encourage the desired responses. If you share classroom space with colleagues, establishing common aims and identifying boundaries will clarify what is possible. At worst, decide what is feasible and portable to bring with you to a session which will help to establish or reinforce the expectations that prevail.

Monitoring the effect of heat and light within the room can have a dramatic effect on the responses and concentration levels of the occupants. The weather outside the building is not controllable, but we can make adjustments in the room to counteract or minimise any detrimental effects. We often think of this as we enter a room but seldom monitor conditions through the session.

Displays

We know, as teachers, that displays can be used to meet a variety of demands. They may be designed to brighten an area, to highlight a particular concept, to bring together work on a theme, to reinforce previous learning, to stimulate interest in a new theme or to provide an opportunity for individual learning in an interactive way. Behaviourally, displays are a significant tool in the classroom. They set the expectations of presentation by giving the opportunity to show or teach the variety of ways in which items can be enhanced through careful mounting and creativity. The value which adults place on presentation of work and the response the pupils receive to their contributions, will impact on their view of themselves as well as their work. Actions speak louder than words, therefore ensuring that all pupils are supported to produce contributions is essential. Once displays are complete they need to be referred to, so that maximum benefit is gained from the effort. Highlighting with pupils the additional elements of planning, negotiating, learning new presentation skills, co-operating and appreciating the work of others, will reinforce the behavioural achievement experienced as a part of the process.

Furniture

Behaviourally, the placing of classroom furniture will have a significant effect. The key is to identify the practical requirements and placing of resources to match the activities and the desired behaviours. If a lot of movement is needed, narrow pathways provide opportunity for jostling, minimising the distance to be travelled reduces the opportunity for inappropriate behaviour. Basic considerations about pupils being able to see whiteboards, illustrations, etc., need to be regularly reviewed and monitored. The most successful arrangements will be a balance between the desired amount of movement and minimising levels of disruption. It can be a surprising experience to try out the pathways we have created ourselves, when the pupils are *in situ* to ensure that theory and practice are balanced.

Final decisions on the furniture will be related to the placing of resources. Having made judgements about the kind of classroom we want to create we will have considered whether basic requirements of pens, pencils, paper etc will be collected by individuals or distributed. Either way the storing of equipment needs to be appropriate to our decision. The implications of thirty pupils collecting a pencil from a central container are obvious! Less obvious maybe are the minor irritations of disagreements over who will distribute equipment or the importance of not being left with the shortest pencil. Ensuring the availability of appropriate resources and foreseeing the possible difficulties will minimise the effect of such challenges.

Some classrooms do not lend themselves to creative arrangements of furniture. We need to keep it as simple as possible. Large numbers of pupils mean little space, which is where we need to ensure that our physical organisation of the room complements our teaching style and the activities we wish to take place in the room. If we wish, or need, a lot of movement around the room we need to organise spacious pathways and carefully place equipment. The pathways around the room are spaces in which there is opportunity for disruptive physical behaviours. By considering the need for and type of movement, you can influence the opportunity for inappropriate behaviours. If we wish pupils to be static, we need to provide equipment within arms reach, or have a set routine for distributing equipment, which is speedy and efficient.

It may seem that the obvious is being stated, or that there is unnecessary attention to detail. However, it is not until we study our classroom in this detail, that we begin to realise that behaviour is all about detail.

Finally, monitoring the effect of any changes we make to the physical environment will help to clarify how to maintain improvement in the behavioural responses of both pupils and adults. An environment where we are able to access what we need, see what is happening, feel comfortable and safe provides optimum opportunity to concentrate on the task in hand. The difficulty is that each individual requires different amounts of each ingredient to fulfil their needs. The challenge then is to find the common ground and develop a culture of compromise and tolerance in our classroom community.

8 The reflective practitioner
Considering the whole class environment

As teachers, we often consider things which may have gone wrong in a lesson, but seldom identify why things have gone well in the same way. Clarifying what was different, to allow improved behaviour or engagement, can help us to take preventative action in the future. Sometimes it is the simplest things which are overlooked, changing seating arrangements, giving responsibility, having tasks ready for pupil entry to class. Each change will have an effect on adult and pupil behaviour. Ideally, working with a colleague through brief reflective discussions about class responses, on a regular basis, we are able to bring observations to a conscious level, which may have passed unrecognised. Sharing ideas about the motivation for particular behaviours can inform our own responses and understanding of situations.

Effect of teacher behaviour

The single most powerful influence in any classroom is the teacher. Again, we can use this knowledge to inform our action or leave things to develop of their own accord. Research indicates that positive relationships between teacher and pupil, significantly influence their learning and behavioural responses. As teachers, we set the tone for the atmosphere of the classroom. We do this on both a daily basis and as an on-going process. We have considered many issues about learning about our pupils' behaviour, but it is essential to realise that they will be learning about our behaviour as well. Part of the process of the establishment phase is about getting to know each other. We do this by trying out what happens if we respond in a particular way to a situation. If we are clear about the key messages we wish to convey then we can use these to inform the tone of our responses.

Personal knowledge of our own behaviour

We can take positive action more quickly, if we know the situations which make us anxious, and our likely response. This can ensure that we manage situations rather than allow them to escalate. Devising a plan of action and even a script, can prevent an emotional hijack of the situation. This will allow us to view the situation with an element of detachment and maximise the opportunity for behavioural learning. Acknowledging the fact that we have different tolerance levels for different pupils can help to clarify our own effective strategies. From this skills base, we begin to add to our behaviour toolbox by building new strategies for particular situations.

Personal knowledge of pupil behaviour

We can gather strategies from many sources, by accident and design, from colleagues and from books. The selection of the right strategy for the right pupil in the right situation is your professional judgement. The decision is made based on knowledge of the particular pupil and context. From our experience, we are able to predict likely responses and motivations for particular behaviours.

Individual baseline

As with learning, we have no option but to begin from where the pupil or class is, at this point in time. Clarifying what they can achieve in a behavioural sense enables us to acknowledge that some learning has taken place and gain some awareness of the timescale of that learning. With this information, we are able to consider the next priority in the short and long term.

Identifying what works

From our experience of the pupil, we can then find examples where their behavioural responses have been most appropriate. By considering why things worked better in these instances, we can formulate a hypothesis about motivation and triggers which give rise to identified behaviours. When considering lesson planning, we are skilled at breaking major concepts into manageable steps for learning. By being clear about what needs to be learned in order for the pupil to access classroom learning, we change the frame in which we view the behaviour. It is less likely to be taken as a personal slight but more as a need for new learning.

Building a hypothesis

This does not need to be a complex and lengthy process, it may only consist of a mental note, that attention seeking is the main motivator during the initial stages of a task. The strategy could then be to provide positive attention and support to ensure initial engagement with the task. This prevents the need for the pupil to indulge in any attention-seeking behaviour at this time. Monitoring the responses will allow refinement of the hypothesis. For example, eliminating the need for this attention seeking may highlight a lack of understanding of instructions preventing a smooth beginning to the task.

Will general class strategies be enough?

Particularly in the establishment phase, our strategies will be formulated with the class as a whole in mind. These strategies will be used to influence group behaviour rather than individual behaviour. As the majority responds, individuals will identify themselves as needing further teaching to support their ability to participate in the class community.

As each strategy is employed, we need to identify when the strategy should be reviewed. This should give enough time for progress, but not so long that we are flogging a dead horse. If the strategy is not effective, it is most likely that we need to review our original hypothesis. All strategies work, but they may not give rise to the response that we intended. By using the response observed to inform our hypothesis, we can build a more precise strategy. The more precise the strategy the more likely that the resultant behaviour will meet our expectations.

Acknowledging success

In order to make best use of a strategy we must acknowledge the success and give feedback to maintain the improved behaviour. If we have been giving specific praise for beginning a work task appropriately until this becomes the norm, making no comment will allow things to drift back to the original response. The intensity of specific praise needed to maintain the appropriate behaviour, is less than is needed to encourage a new behaviour. The theme of consistency should be evident throughout the behavioural calendar but it will be challenged most during the establishment phase.

Mobilising support

Before considering mobilising support, we need to be clear about the type of support which will be effective in any particular situation. It is often tempting to think only of defining support as an additional adult involved in one-to-one work. Not only is this not always effective, but it can be counterproductive if used inappropriately. By working through the process previously described, we are more likely to be able to identify appropriate requirements for support. This will then inform the type of support, which will effect the desired behaviour change.

Careful planning of our own input with particular pupils will minimise their difficulty and prevent a considerable number of possible disruptions to learning. Planning to address the three preferred learning styles of aural, kinesthetic and visual will increase engagement in learning. Interest boosting at key points during the lesson will maintain engagement. Each of these strategies while increasing optimum use of learning time, will also reduce opportunity for off-task, low-level disruption. Essentially, strategies should be considered at different levels to meet the level of behavioural need. There is no need to use a sledgehammer to crack a nut.

Further support can be provided through careful use of seating arrangements, management of work partners for particular tasks. This can be extended to specific peer support. Using this technique needs to be carefully taught and organised. Pupils need to be involved in identifying the type of support they require and are able to deliver in particular circumstances. This can be most effective in a community where there is an acceptance that at some stage every member will need assistance, including the adults.

The concepts of giving and receiving support are essential to harmonious relationships. Surprisingly for many of us, accepting is much more difficult than giving support. This is particularly true of pupils and adults with significant difficulties. A successful supportive relationship requires those involved to play roles which involve the admission, if only to themselves, that they need help. To be able to accept this we need to believe that the admission will not be followed by ridicule or stereotyping. As teachers, we can highlight the fact that all members of the class community are able to play both roles successfully. This takes careful management to ensure that particular pupils are not always expected to receive support. There is an inherent street cred within school cultures to be able to give support. Some pupils are excluded from this experience because they are viewed as having nothing to offer. The difficulty is more likely to be related to lack of knowledge about how to give support and lack of opportunity to practise the skills.

As a part of our lesson planning, differentiation of tasks is now commonplace, either on a group or individual basis. Being able to provide appropriate, achievable tasks for the range of abilities represented within a class is a major challenge. It is also though one of the most significant factors in supporting a pupil's behaviour. The other major factor is the teacher's relationship with both the class and individual pupils. In our initial clarification of our understanding of the role of the teacher, we highlighted the messages we wanted to convey. If these messages include interest in pupils as individuals, concern about their progress, willingness to listen and willingness to share involvement in seeking solutions to difficulties, then we will be offering the most effective support available.

Using colleague support in planning and as support for particular strategies, will increase our confidence in managing specific difficulties. Arrangements for pupils to complete tasks in another class or show work to colleagues can be powerful motivators if used appropriately. Such strategies are clearly based in detailed knowledge of individual pupils, but they can be built into the value systems of the class community. Pupils will be aware of hierarchy within the department or school, if the adults value colleagues' opinions, pupils will gain prestige from praise from those colleagues also. If additional adults are working within the class, it is essential that these elements are the basis for the working relationship which should then become a triangle of support.

Having adults to support in class is often viewed as a luxury even today. But it can be an additional stress in managing the class community. Clarification of expectations of how the support can be delivered is essential and roles and responsibilities must be clear. We all work more effectively if we understand what we are expected to do. The support must be focussed on the times and situations in which the pupil is in greatest need. It must also be delivered in the manner that the pupil is best able to accept.

Personal support systems

Whatever the identified difficulty the principles which guide mobilising support should include early intervention, providing clear evidence of response to strategies used, needs-led focus and regular monitoring of progress. Moderating decisions and strategies with colleagues will aid equitable, needs-led, distribution of resources and ensure that all other forms of support have been attempted before additional adult time is required.

Our expectations of what can be achieved with support needs to be realistic and achievable. This view needs to be shared with all involved adults so that joint aims and goals are identified. Learning of any curriculum area is often a rocky path which is even more pronounced for the behavioural curriculum.

In considering what support is available, we need also to think about our own personal support systems. We previously identified times of the school year, which we found more difficult. These are the times when we will be significantly challenged by the behaviour of others. They are therefore also the times when we need to increase our stress-busting activities, whatever they may be, more exercise, talk, music etc. By being proactive in this way, we are able to maintain our perspective of pupil behaviour in the context of our initial behaviour plan rather than feeling that all is lost and no progress has been made. This also involves balancing teacher time and realising that we can't fix everything, but we can make a difference.

Without doubt, the teacher dictates the climate of the classroom, therefore reflecting honestly about sessions in behavioural terms is a very efficient way of improving the interactions which take place. If this reflection process can take place with the other adults involved in the class, so much the better.

9 Consolidation phase

Considering behaviour from the pupil's perspective

The consolidation phase begins around the end of the first and beginning of the second term. By this stage, the class community has established a system of relationships and hierarchy. The majority of pupils will behave appropriately on the majority of occasions. Equally, those who have difficulty with behavioural learning or are otherwise motivated will have clearly identified themselves. We need to be careful to acknowledge the needs of both groups at this stage. We will be particularly aware of the latter group because of their contribution to our frustration and stress levels.

The original behaviour action plan can now be revised, acknowledging the progress made. In the same way that we revise curriculum plans, there is a need to reflect on whether progress is as we expected and if not why not. This does not mean looking for a hook on which to hang the blame, but to build on strengths and access appropriate advice and strategies to make further progress.

As part of our reflection during the consolidation phase, we should also consider and review the impact of school systems, teaching styles and organisation. Often the routines and structures in school have a supportive effect on pupil behaviour. Sometimes it does not. Looking for time and context patterns of inappropriate behaviour can point to a system which encourages deterioration of behaviour. For example, in some schools pupils who behave inappropriately during break times stand in line in a corridor. Pupils may identify this as the best place to be on a wet day, inside with all your mates. Looking at systems from the pupil's perspective can be very illuminating and shadowing particular pupils can highlight obvious difficulties. One situation worth exploring is to compare the variety of behaviours exhibited by specific pupils with different teachers. Also the changes in behaviour during practical subjects, hall times, in large classrooms, small classrooms, in large groups, small groups, etc. We are all susceptible to different feelings engendered by the amount of space available to us.

It is equally important to give feedback to the group of pupils who have achieved or exceeded the targets set. A review of the establishment phase discussions and displays about behaviour will focus attention on appropriate behaviours which have become an accepted part of classroom life. It will also give an opportunity to reflect on how difficult or easy it has been to achieve these targets.

There is an expectation that pupils have considerable knowledge about how a classroom works. They are aware of nuances of behavioural limits and can interpret a variety of responses. In every class, there is a group of pupils who are skilled and respond appropriately within the variety of interactions in which they are involved. These pupils have had positive relationships with adults previously. They have developed confidence and belief in their own worth and ability. We each bring a wealth of preconceived ideas and expectations to every interaction. In our own interpretation of any situation, we select elements which resonate with our established beliefs. If our beliefs and experiences are positive, these will be enhanced further. However, if they are negatively framed they will be further entrenched.

The role of the teacher

The role of the teacher in the classroom is fraught with difficulty. The position can be a focus for much external criticism and judgement. Everyone has been to school, therefore everyone knows how the job should be done. This overlooks the increasing complexity of the teaching, learning interaction and the place of schools in society. As a profession we need to resist the temptation to meet today's problems with yesterday's solutions.

To objectively decide on our individual definition of the role of the teacher, we need to be sufficiently self-aware to be able to own up to our motivation for becoming teachers. We need to base our professionalism on increasing our self-awareness and developing our communication skills to enable us to enhance the learning of the pupils we teach. The first test of our professionalism is to be challenged with the question of what is the major purpose of the job of teaching. In these days of mountains of paperwork, increased public accountability and governmental pressure it is easier to become side-tracked into feeling disgruntled by claims that we are responsible for society's ills or believing that it is our remit to remedy all these identified ills. Our job is to teach, but to accomplish this we are becoming increasingly aware of the intricacies and complexities of the teaching and learning processes.

In developing our views of what is involved in the reality of teaching, we must set our expectations within the realms of what is possible. There is a commonly held fantasy that teaching is an easy job and all that is required is to present appropriate work and pupils will learn, this is not true. Consider the last time that you learnt something; concentrate on what enhanced the learning for you, what was it about the 'teacher' which helped you to learn, what helped you to retain the learning and to apply it independently. In working through this process you can gradually identify your individual learning style. Inevitably, this will be based mainly on visual, kinesthetic or aural presentation. If we find a particular aspect of the learning process difficult, we rely even more heavily on our preferred learning style, our pupils do the same.

As teachers, we collect an enormous amount of information and knowledge about our pupils. Pressure is increasing on the time available to deliver greater quantity of curriculum content. Knowledge that we have acquired about our pupils, which would enable accelerated learning, is rapidly losing status. As a consequence, we overlook the opportunity to reflect on the knowledge that we have about schools as learning environments, the teaching process, the optimum conditions for learning and predictable elements of the academic year. With the opportunity to reflect on situations comes the ability to identify patterns. This provides the opportunity to predict events and plan to deal proactively with a situation or better still to prevent difficulties occurring.

From the establishment phase we will have an awareness of progress in terms of individual, group and class behaviour. In order to secure and build on this we need to clearly reflect this progress to pupils. We can then set out our expectations and targets for the consolidation phase of the year. If we are specific enough about setting targets we will be able to clearly evidence progress. Our reflection of progress will be differentiated for groups and individuals as appropriate. Where necessary we will work with pupils to construct small step targets with short timescales and achievable rewards. To increase the power of this process it is useful to share both achievement and targets with other significant adults. Where possible this should be with adults from home but it may be as effective in some situations to use colleagues in school.

Pupils are now regularly involved in setting their own curriculum targets and with support can be introduced to appropriate targets for behaviour. Often the need is to reduce the demands of pupil-generated targets to increase the opportunity for success within a reasonable timescale. Using accurate baseline information will help to make this a realistic process. Some pupils will identify impossible targets or be unable to acknowledge their success. These are indicators that the pupil feels they are unsuccessful, do not deserve reward, or are not as good as others. Such feelings are directly related to self-esteem. We can support such pupils to build on their successes through a gradual, low key acknowledgement of specific progress. Although pupils may be able to accept our identification of success. it will take longer for them to respond positively to our praise, or to identify their own success.

Any type or system of reward can be used, but for it to be effective, it must be valued by the individual members of the class and school community.

Routines patterns and triggers

A focus for review of our hypothesis about motivation can be to monitor and identify the triggers for the behaviours. Often we, in the teaching context feel that challenging behaviours have no trigger. They are completely unprovoked, but typical of the pupils concerned. This is a process which allows us to disassociate ourselves from any responsibility for addressing the behaviour. The reality is however, that there is a trigger, but we have no opportunity to have seen the start of the episode. In re-examining the situation, we can collect evidence from a variety of sources. A key contributor will, of course, be the pupil, who initially may not be clear about triggers, but will be able to work through some hypothesis in partnership with you.

The acknowledgement of the difficulty in a non-confrontational manner gives the opportunity for a problem-solving approach aside from the incident. The situation then has a context of cognitive activity rather than pure emotional expression. This is not to say that talking through the situation once will solve the problem, but it will teach a positive and purposeful approach to managing behaviour. This is an approach that can be used by individual pupils and adults.

Target setting, sharing concern, case conferencing

We glibly talk about target setting as a powerful tool in learning. Unless the target setting process is seen as important as the actual writing of the target, they will have little effect. The target 'I will sit quietly when the teacher is speaking', given to a pupil is unlikely to have any effect on its own. It is not the target which changes the behaviour, but the involvement of others, the supportive relationship which can develop, the awareness of difficulty and an attempt to do something to help in a pragmatic way.

A target which highlights difficulty without providing the teaching to remedy the situation, figuratively pushes the pupil away. It communicates to them that they are failing, increasingly isolated and in some way inadequate. It is quite a different approach to acknowledge the presenting behaviour through a statement with as little emotion as possible, then to share possible small steps which can become the basis for a realistic target to support and evidence progress. Consider your own learning, in approaching any area of learning it would be easy to list one hundred things which you did not know or could not do within the topic. But that approach would not progress your learning as much as identifying your existing learning followed by the next achievable step.

By reflecting back the learning we have achieved, we are able to have confidence in the possibility of success. We also feel that we are not alone in our learning, that we have a guide whom we can approach to share our successes and failures. Our level of confidence in our guide will be dependent on previous experience and will have to be tested. Initially, we may offload responsibility for our learning on to our guide. If they are not interested in our success or difficulty then why should we bother, the guide's behaviour reinforces our previous experience of being let down by those in authority. We are left with the view that it is easier not to change because it is all too hard and nobody really cares anyway.

Development of such a level of involvement with parents and carers is an investment for the future. It supports both the educational career of the pupil but also the foundations of lifelong learning. In addition, such a whole school approach is particularly supportive of the individual teacher who needs to address difficult issues with parents and carers. It is worth considering any parent consultation meeting from the perspective of each individual present. This provides an opportunity to make the best of each meeting, even the most difficult. Again it is a situation where prevention is better than cure, planning and preparation can avert misunderstandings developing into a breakdown of communications. Initial decisions include:

> Who needs to be present?
> Where can the meeting be held?
> Is the appropriate furniture available?
> Can refreshments be offered?
> Who will chair the meeting?
> Who will take the minutes?
> What issues need to be discussed?
> In what ways are people likely to react to the issues?

In what ways can you best manage this behaviour?
In what ways can you welcome those attending the meeting?
In what ways can you support those attending to feel comfortable?
In what ways can you ensure that everyone contributes?
How can you ensure that everyone feels that they have been heard?

Using a baseline

We can identify a way forward by formulating baseline information about the intensity, frequency and context of the inappropriate behaviours. This will help us to maintain a realistic view and measure any changes. It can also often challenge our anecdotal belief that the behaviour happens all the time, in every context. Finally, it will enable us to consider realistic targets which will highlight progress.

When targets are set with agreed rewards and consequences, it is important to identify a review date. This will maintain interest, give a focus for achievement and opportunity to amend the system, if it is not having the desired effect. The review date needs to allow sufficient time for the system to be consistently applied. If targets are set appropriately some rewards should be gained quickly to ensure confidence in the possibility of success. Nothing succeeds like success; it is the best motivator in the majority of situations.

The sharing process

Having established the baseline, we need to acknowledge the difficulty with those involved. This will obviously include discussion with the pupils but should also involve, parents/carers and specific colleagues. The colleagues will be identified by either their role within the school or the level of support they are able to extend to us. This support may be a critical friend role for ourselves, the pupil, or involvement in agreed practical strategies to manage the behaviour. Collegiate support at this stage is also important to moderate decisions and judgements about the behaviour. Sharing with pupils the use of target setting from a positive basis, discussing strategies and prompts will help to involve them in the process and can often introduce some novel ideas about supporting each other.

Reframing the aspirations, boundaries, entitlements and consequences

Having come this far, we can identify improvements we would like to make during this phase. We will have established judgements and stereotypical views of the characters in the class community. The challenge now is to make changes which will create the opportunity for reframing the relationships. We may be able to use new grouping arrangements or discussion situations to highlight individual strengths. This can then be used to identify strengths which individuals wish to develop through targets.

Some of the relationships in the class will not be so positive. This will be true of pupils and adults. We will have developed a pattern of expectations and responses which are difficult to change. We can probably recite the scripts without the person being present. In order to develop behavioural learning around the relationship someone needs to take the adult role to change the dialogue. Changing the dialogue will significantly affect the presenting behaviour and the subsequent response. Rather than the script leading to stalemate or confrontation a new wording or tone can shift the emphasis to behavioural learning. For example:

> Why haven't you got a pencil?
> *Cos I lost it!*
> Don't speak to me like that!
> *Like what, I didn't do anything, you're always picking on me!*
> You know perfectly well what I mean! Anymore of that and you will be
>   out of the class.

Alternative script:

> You don't have a pencil. Use this one, return it to me at the end of the
>   session.
> [At the end of the session.]
> It is important that you have the correct equipment for each lesson. What
>   do you need to do to ensure that you have a pencil next time?
> *Get a new one.*
> If you get a new one, what can you do to make sure you do not lose it?
> *Buy more than one, keep it somewhere safe.*

The dialogue may involve rewards and consequences if appropriate.

By changing the wording we have changed the tone, and also the focus. Rather than a conflict about something which has been said, it becomes an opportunity to move the situation forward. The responsibility is also with the pupil who has the opportunity to suggest possible solutions. This dialogue can be extended to finding ways of supporting the pupil to accept responsibility for organising their own equipment in other contexts.

It should not be overlooked that apparently insignificant problems can be indicators of more important difficulties. For example, finding tasks too difficult, lack of confidence with basic skills, poor peer relationships. By the time we get to the consolidation phase, persistent behaviours are worth re-examining and the hypothesis about motivation amended.

By this stage in the year patterns of behaviour have become more entrenched but can still be changed. The way individuals respond to each other is informed by their perception of how relationships work. Some of us present different sets of behaviours according to the role we are playing. Others are able to be congruent in the messages they give, but adjusting the delivery to match the context.

Variety of ways of acknowledging progress

If we define progress as positive change we need to be able to acknowledge and give evidence of such change. Some individuals have difficulty in identifying their own progress or gaining positive feelings from making progress. As teachers giving positive feedback of progress and achievement is one of our most powerful tools. We can use a variety of systems and mechanisms to acknowledge the positive changes. It is useful to identify those available within your own school and class before deciding how or when you would apply them.

For example there could be some or all of the following:

> verbal praise
> smile
> written comments/symbols
> stickers
> rewards charts to be ticked/coloured, etc
> sharing of positive feedback with a wider audience, adults or pupils
> photographic evidence
> achievement display
> achievement book
> certificates
> verbal report to parent/carer
> letter to parent/carer
> individual praise
> group praise
> peer feedback
> achievement prize
> activity reward
> privileges
> responsibilities

Once the possible means of acknowledging progress in your school/class have been identified, it is possible to place them in hierarchical order. They can then be matched to appropriate situations in which they would be awarded.

Dangerous times

In our original behaviour plan we will have predicted times in the year when behaviour will be significantly affected. This may include seasonal, climatic or school activities. By the time we are in the consolidation phase we know our pupils well enough to accurately predict their responses to most situations. It is important to use this knowledge positively to give pupils the best possible chance to access the opportunities in school. We can then prepare them for the impending events as appropriate. High levels of excitement are likely to be the issue, for example prior to a school fair, a snowy day etc. The teaching involved would centre around awareness and identification of those feelings. This needs to be followed by acknowledgement of the resultant observable behaviours. Finally, consideration should be given to acceptable ways of expressing the excitement. After the event there would then be feedback of the positive aspects of the observable behaviours during the event.

Allowing pupils to share a problem-solving approach to self-control and behaviour management is not only about coping with a specific event. It is also about learning about ourselves, our responses and the effect our behaviour has on others. This is more than school learning, it is lifelong learning. As adults we are not yet able to manage our behaviour to best effect in all situations yet we expect pupils to do so. You know your pupils, they know you. In order to protect against complacency, take time to reflect, identify and celebrate success. This will enable you to compare behaviour from the establishment phases and review the class rules. Consider with pupils the ways in which the rules have influenced the classroom community. Sharing perceptions about what happened if rules were broken, can be a useful starting point for redrafting and reteaching the expectations.

One of the key points for discussion will be the difficulties of maintaining consistency of response in line with the agreed class rules. The process of reflecting on the behavioural development of the community is a valuable tool for teaching about tolerance and compromise. It also defines realistic timescales for changes in the group behaviour accepting the influence of external factors. From this discussion, it may be possible for pupils to design a method of recording the progress made and appropriate ways to celebrate.

10 Transitions
Identifying areas of increased concern

It is a reality that for those of us in difficult schools, the management of behaviour is a relentless struggle. We are constantly required to evaluate and refine our strategies, and to search for new and innovative measures to stem what sometimes seems like an ever-rising tide. Nor can we ever relax our vigilance if we are to minimise disruption and anti-social behaviour. It is most important that all staff feel safe and supported when exercising their authority within the parameters of the behaviour action plan. If staff feel uneasy or exposed, they may be reluctant to try to operate and articulate the school's position. This can result in a weakened and fragmented response to disruption. Youngsters will be quick to point out to you when you tackle them about whatever infringement they are involved in, that they passed Mr So-and-so and he didn't say anything.

The establishment phase will result in the majority of youngsters getting the message, but there will be a significant minority who need more than the usual reminders. To keep the majority conforming, and to make inroads into the minority, requires constant vigilance and constant periods of renewed focus in conjunction with a well-publicised system of rewards. We will become aware of where the message needs to be reinforced. The staff behaviour forum has a role to play here, in identifying where the message is being diluted and in providing the impetus to tackle these areas. There are positives to look for here, in identifying those areas that need extra attention we shouldn't lose sight of what we've achieved. We may have the majority of our youngsters in uniform, for example, we may have the majority of our youngsters on time every day, and countless other plusses that can be obscured by the serious disruption of the few.

It is important, however, to continually press home the school's behaviour action plan. The reward system must be in place to reinforce compliant behaviour, and must be rigorously employed and highly visible. Good behaviour must be rewarded and be seen to be rewarded, just as poor behaviour must be seen to be beyond tolerance. As the term progresses there can be no doubt that compliance will slip unless constantly 'tweaked' by all the processes the school has at its disposal. The behaviour action plan at this stage must reflect this and all the efforts of the staff should be steered towards the identified objectives.

Blitzing

Having identified our successes, it then becomes necessary to identify those areas that require extra or renewed effort. If we wish to focus on a particular aspect of indiscipline, we must use all the processes available to us to seek to reduce this. Organised campaigns against whatever it is we are trying to reduce, must involve informing our students, informing their parents, assemblies, spot-checks, rewards, increased staff vigilance, a corporate and solid response from the entire faculty. Such 'pushes' require energy and optimism in the dark days of winter and staff fatigue.

The behaviour action plan must create 'protected' space for the deliberations of the staff behaviour forum and also create the expectation that the forum will communicate with all staff to pinpoint areas of concern and provide useful strategies to deal with those concerns.

This transitional stage should be characterised therefore by identification of areas of increased concern, and by the selection of a series of strategies that can address those concerns. The raft of rewards for compliant behaviours must be attainable for all our students at some point in the school year. There can be tensions amongst staff concerning the operation of rewards. Some of us may believe very firmly that virtue is its own reward, and that we should not reward youngsters who constantly misbehave, and who are only occasionally compliant. To take such a view is to misunderstand the purpose of reward as part of a regime to improve behaviour.

Of course, the youngster who has perfect attendance, keeps perfect time, is always compliant and pleasant must be rewarded. There are, however, powerful and intrinsic rewards for them in the constant warmth and approval they will undoubtedly experience from their teachers, and in the pride that the school takes in them. They have the emotional security that makes the educational experience a positive one. They are also entitled to all the extrinsic rewards the school has at its disposal, making them 'twice blessed', and why not?

Using rewards to increase compliance and to encourage the desired behaviours in our students has very little to do with the time-honoured model of school prize-giving ceremonies. Rewarding good behaviour is quite simply the best way to bring about a repeat of that behaviour. Given what we know about the way the emotional brain responds, we can no longer regard this as the 'weaker' option to the punishment of poor behaviour.

Transitional phase – a pupil's perspective

The transitional phase for our pupils starts around Easter each academic year. Although the issues may also be around at other times related to exams, choosing schools and other unsettling times. The transition phase for pupils is about moving on and facing change. The predominant emotion is one of anxiety. The anxiety is evident for both pupils and adults at this time. One of the major influences on behaviour is anxiety. It is the most difficult emotion for an individual to manage. Even when feeling angry, there is a significant element of anxiety that affect our ability to move on from our expression of anger.

There are many reasons for us to feel anxious, some are logical and in proportion to the issues, others are not. Anxiety is a very personal response in that there are many situations which make us anxious, but have no effect on those around us. There is nothing wrong in feeling any particular emotion, the crucial factor is the way in which the feeling is expressed. To be able to manage our own feelings we need to be able identify early signs of our anxiety. This enables us to have the best possible chance to manage our responses in the situation.

Bridging the changes to the next class/year group/school

Having identified that transition anxieties are related to change, we can consider ways to work with the change to make it less anxious-making. Often there is a direct relationship between the amount of information we have and the level of anxiety we feel. Through discussion with pupils we can explore ways in which we have survived change in the past. Part of this process is about identifying the personal strategies which helped us to cope. It is also about addressing our fear of the unknown through accurate information. For example, identifying similarities between this class or year group with the next, or identifying things which will change for the better in our view.

Reflecting on how we have been able to assimilate similar new situations in the past also allows us to compare the impact of familiarity. On a purely physical level we can use specific relaxation techniques to help us to deal with the physical symptoms to alleviate the intensity of feeling. This then gives us the opportunity to maintain our feelings at a level which allows us to continue functioning in spite of the emotion.

It is as important to support parents and carers to move on from one teacher to another as it is to support pupils. The response of parents and carers to school directly affects pupils. This is particularly noticeable on a daily basis with younger pupils. Often older pupils are better at masking their feelings. Parents and carers who find it difficult to make positive relationships with individuals in perceived authority roles, will inevitably find it hard to leave one relationship for another. Their anxiety level will rise and they will express this in a variety of ways.

11   Planning spirit lifters
Incentives for good behaviour

Without a doubt there are certain times within the academic year when stresses and tensions rise. These tensions may be associated with seasonal changes, dark days grinding slowly towards the end of a long and arduous term. We invariably associate these times with increased indiscipline as tiredness invariably takes its toll on staff and pupils. Because we have a perception of increased indiscipline, *ipso facto* there is – ask any member of the senior management team of any school. They can pinpoint those times when their in trays are overflowing with discipline referrals or increased numbers of pupils sent to them. It will undoubtedly feel like the wrong time to be giving these awful pupils any sort of treat, but in fact it is absolutely the right time and does have a pay-off for all the stakeholders, staff, pupils and parents. What we seek to do is to positively influence the behavioural culture at those times when it is most endangered.

The benefits for the pupils are obviously first and foremost to provide a bit of fun, to lighten the day. It also provides them with the opportunity of being viewed in a different light. For example, the worst behaved may turn out to be a brilliant break dancer perhaps, the surliest pupil may display an unaccustomed smile. It provides an opportunity for pupils to demonstrate commitment. Manning the roll-a-penny stall for the whole morning of the mini-fête without complaint, for example. It may provide pupils with the opportunity to show previously unrecognised strengths or untapped spheres of interest.

For teachers seeing their charges behaving differently, many with obvious enjoyment goes a long way towards changing perceptions of doom and gloom. As a group we can refocus our shared values in the very planning of such events. We may well see each other in a different light and as a consequence find a team spirit where hitherto we imagined that none existed. We can find increased confidence in colleagues, and they in you, by a collaborative and well-realised event. Such events undoubtedly present as a challenge and are always tiring. It is a positive stress however, and very often a shared experience.

A successful stress-lifter, however small, brings its own sense of a worthwhile effort, regardless of how strenuous that effort may have been. A successful run up, a well managed event, a sense of completion and closure when it is all over can re-invigorate a jaded teaching staff. Obviously, the more ambitious the project the more rigorous the planning. With nothing left to chance, the only spontaneity will hopefully be the enjoyment of all on the day. Photographic or video evidence of any stress-busting activity will prolong the feel-good factor for all concerned.

Spirit-lifters do not need to be extravagant or ambitious, although it is great to have one event in the year which is both of these things. The important elements are that they should boost interest levels, focus positive attention and generally lift the atmosphere. Spirit-lifters can be anything that does any or all of the above, such as:

- Music playing in the classroom
- Giving ourselves a round of applause
- Good news letters to go home
- Well done visit from the head teacher
- A walk on a dry day
- A class mini-fête
- A charity push
- Dressing-up days
- Multicultural events, flags day, 'eat the world'

Resourceful and imaginative teachers will be able to think of any number of events, knowing as they do the needs of their own institution.

A caveat

Having drafted our behaviour plan within the context of the existing whole school ethos and approaches, we go on to consider the ongoing detail of daily life in our class community. The majority of pupils within our class will participate in the majority of our lessons on the majority days of the academic year, but there will never be a day when:

- Every pupil enters our class desperate to learn what we will teach
- Every pupil is happy, relaxed and concerned about our welfare
- Every pupil follows every instruction correctly
- Every pupil completes every task correctly
- Every pupil thanks us for our time and effort in teaching them
- Every parent/carer thanks us for teaching their children.

If we know this is not going to happen, telling ourselves we have failed when it doesn't, is a daily punishment we can do without. Setting our expectations at an achievable level is an essential part of managing our own behaviour and stress. We seldom articulate such targets, even to ourselves, but we frequently indulge in a negatively focussed review of the day. The consequence of this is either that we accept the associated blame or look for others to accuse. If we direct the blame towards the pupils, this will directly affect our relationship with them in a negative way. Feelings of anger begin to grow as these pupils prevent us from achieving super-teacher status in our own eyes. Alternatively, the anger is that the pupils are responsible for deskilling and sapping our confidence. Being able to identify such emotions in our self can be a painful process, but it can be easily remedied by reframing our review of the day in a positive way. Naming the successes sounds too easy but when it becomes our usual perspective we are more likely to be able to sustain a realistic perspective. Using statements naming what individual and groups of pupils did appropriately can give us evidence that it wasn't quite the disastrous day we originally thought.

This is one of the situations where it is advantageous to be able to identify our emotions accurately. Often our disappointment and frustration are really expressions of tiredness. The tiredness however can engender feelings of helplessness and depression if we continue to talk ourselves down. Positively acknowledging a difficult day and feelings of tiredness allow us to reflect on what was achieved and possibilities for raising energy levels. Otherwise, we begin the next situation with feelings of dread and reluctance. For a guide to realistic expectations it can be useful to clarify what observable features indicate to you that it is a good, moderate, difficult day. Updating these on a termly or half-termly basis can also give you feedback about the behavioural progress of the class community.

It would be very easy to focus our considerations of behavioural issues around inappropriate behaviour, but the reality is that behaviour encompasses everything we do and everything we say. Every behaviour has a purpose and a message. Some individuals are more adept at identifying the intentions and effects of their behaviours than others. This is true of both adults and children. In schools we often ask individuals why they have acted in a particular way, in fact we can become quite fixated on the question at times. If we reflect on our own reasons for our behaviours in any detail we begin to see what a difficult question it can be to attempt to answer. Our behaviour is interpreted differently according to our perceived age, stage and the context in which it occurs. For example, it would be reasonable for a toddler to cry and tantrum if unable to have the drink they wanted. This would be viewed differently if it was an adult or if the drink was hot coffee. The toddler does not yet have language or understanding to express their needs and wishes. Adults have a much wider range of communic-ation and manipulation skills to be able to get our needs met. In times of stress or frustration though, we often resort to less sophisticated strategies to express our emotions. For example, we know rationally that we will not make the car start by hitting the steering wheel or kicking the tyre, but we use these actions as an expression of our frustration. We continue to learn about emotional and behavioural literacy throughout life. We make judgements about our own responses, which result in changes and amendments in our behaviour. We use regret and apology to try to change things we have done, we resolve not to repeat them. We are well aware of the theory, we lose our temper with particular people too quickly, we provoke certain behaviours in others with a targeted comment. If we are still learning as adults after all these years of practice, it is unreasonable to expect pupils to be able to assimilate new behavioural learning after one lesson.

The fact remains that the presenting behaviour is giving a message about needs which are unmet. This does not mean that as teachers we are responsible for every pupil's difficulties and have the opportunity to be social worker, friend, mother and father to our pupils. It does mean that we may be able to identify the motivation behind certain behaviours. This will enable us to build a strategy which will allow a more positive engagement within the classroom community.

Conclusion
The role of the teacher

We have explored many of the behavioural issues involved in the complex process of teaching and learning in the school environment. Undoubtedly, there are some which we can influence more than others. If nothing else we are able to consider the pivotal role that we as individual teachers play in the class community. This is also the element over which we have most influence. The role of the teacher in the classroom is fraught with difficulty. The position can be a focus for much external criticism and judgement. Everyone has been to school, therefore everyone knows how the job should be done. This overlooks the increasing complexity of the teaching–learning interaction and the place of schools in society. As a profession, we need to resist the temptation to meet today's problems with yesterday's solutions.

To objectively decide on our individual definition of the role of the teacher, we need to be sufficiently self-aware to be able to own up to our motivation for becoming teachers. We need to base our professionalism on increasing our self-awareness and developing our communication skills to enable us to enhance the learning of the pupils we teach. The first test of our professionalism is to be challenged with the question of what is the major purpose of the job of teaching. In these days of mountains of paperwork, increased public accountability and governmental pressure, it is easier to become side-tracked into feeling disgruntled by claims that we are responsible for society's ills or believing that it is our remit to remedy all these identified ills. Our job is to teach, but to accomplish this we are becoming increasingly aware of the intricacies and complexities of the teaching and learning processes.

Realistic expectations

In developing our views of what is involved in the reality of teaching, we must set our expectations within the realms of what is possible. There is a commonly held fantasy that teaching is an easy job, and that all that is required is to present appropriate work and that pupils will learn. This is not true! Consider the last time that you learnt something; concentrate on what enhanced the learning for you; what was it about the 'teacher' which helped you to learn, what helped you to retain the learning and to apply it independently. In working through this process you can gradually identify your individual learning style. Inevitably, this will be based mainly on visual, kinesthetic or aural presentation. If we find a particular aspect of the learning process difficult, we rely even more heavily on our preferred learning style, and our pupils do the same.

As teachers, we collect an enormous amount of information and knowledge about our pupils. Pressure is increasing on the time available to deliver a greater quantity of curriculum content. Knowledge that we have acquired about our pupils, which would enable accelerated learning, is rapidly losing status. As a consequence, we overlook the opportunity to reflect on the knowledge that we have about schools as learning environments, the teaching process, the optimum conditions for learning and predictable elements of the academic year. With the opportunity to reflect on situations comes the ability to identify patterns. This provides the opportunity to predict events and plan to deal proactively with a situation, or better still, to prevent difficulties occurring.

Dealing with inappropriate behaviour

The management of inappropriate behaviour is an everyday reality for many of us in the teaching profession. It's a never-ending challenge to the well-being of everyone in our classrooms. How we long for the perfect solution, the one that works first time, every time. Such a complex range of factors is at work in the classroom that no such solution exists, or ever could. For the teacher, the classroom is busy and very public. We are highly visible to all the other participants in any event in the classroom, which brings its own vulnerability. The teacher is required to manage the many dimensions of the classroom, the learning and teaching the social and personal interactions, a multiplicity of resources and tasks, all the while giving out verbal prompts and non-verbal signals.

Classroom events can be simultaneous, and with a difficult class, this can seem overwhelming as we try to keep pupils on task. There is a manic fairground game whereby crocodiles pop their heads up at unpredictable locations and time intervals – the object of the game is to smash the heads down with a mallet as fast as possible before the next one pops up. Teaching any class with a large disruptive element feels much like this game – minus the mallets, naturally!

Classrooms can be very unpredictable and therein lies the real stress for the teacher, having struggled to get everyone on task and quiet, a wasp flies in the window for example, and the teacher has to start the whole process again. Much of what happens in the classroom is predictable, however. A thorough knowledge of the age and stage of our pupils can help us in our dealings with them.

Stress levels

Predicting the presenting behaviours goes some way to reducing stress. Planning strategies to overcome them will enhance our sense of being in control. Examination of our own behaviour and reflection on our practice is a crucial element in the management of behaviour in our classrooms.

Behaviour management can never be a quick-fix issue, nor can it be left to chance or to the individual teacher. A consistent, school-wide approach is essential, and such an approach will need constant revision, development and regular fine-tuning. A safety net of staff support is an essential element of a whole school approach, from the informal 'listening ear' through to a structured and planned programme of staff development. The development of a positive, personable, but assertive approach to discipline is a job for the whole establishment and should involve all the stakeholders. In this package, we have set out to explore the behaviours that challenge us all on a daily basis and to suggest ways for schools to meet this challenge.

Whilst acknowledging the difficulties that we as teachers encounter, this package offers a sympathetic, but potent response. It provides an opportunity to examine our practice in a developmental way either individually or ideally as a whole school. The text can serve as background and reminder of the issues exemplified in the INSET sessions. With changing staff groups and changing pupil populations, the issues need to be revisited and applied to the 'new' context. We cannot 'do' behaviour at the beginning of the year and then leave it to develop unguided. The reality is that there are major pressures on INSET time for all schools and priorities will be decided on a school by school basis. But in our opinion, if we reduce the priority of behaviour we will pay a heavy price.

INSET Sessions

The purpose of these INSET sessions is to provide a framework within which behavioural issues can be examined and explored in the individual school context. Ideally they would be used with whole staff groups and the whole school approach developed through all adults involved in the school community. The sessions are based on the four assumptions identified in Chapter 3, namely,

1   The behaviour of teachers influences the behaviour of pupils.

2   Techniques of classroom management can be identified and learned.

3   Teachers must take responsibility for developing their skill.

4   Effective teachers are skilled at minimising problems.

The in-sets in this book are designed to model good pedagogy. The following notes provide prompts for the person leading the sessions to consider in their preparation. In the same way that preparation of a lesson can optimise learning INSET delivery can succeed or fail at this stage. Knowledge of the audience should be used to support learning and predict the range of responses. INSET delivery is most effective when the leader is clear about the role they will play and the messages they wish to communicate. This will include the more subtle messages, such as a positive approach to behaviour, a problem-solving view of difficulties, response to contributions from others, as well as the key points of each session. The messages will be most effectively communicated if they are congruently applied.

The sessions are designed to last approximately $1\frac{1}{2}$ to 2 hours.

The INSET leader should consider the following in their preparation:

Appropriate materials ⟶	Congruent with learners' needs
A range of different activities ⟶	Suited to each of the learning 'comfort zones'
A personable and purposeful delivery ⟶	To accommodate the emotional needs of the learners

This personal audit will help to clarify preparation decisions which will support effective delivery of the sessions.

How do I want it to be?	How do I achieve this?
I want it to be physically comfortable	Use a suitably comfortable venue Check seating arrangements Choose an appropriate time of day Offer refreshments (If none of the above is possible, acknowledge and share the difficulties)
I want it to reflect expertise	With well-prepared resources Well-prepared technology Sufficient materials for all participants Demonstrate knowledge of the institution Confident presentation and mastery of the materials Setting schedules and sticking to them Smoothly managed transitions between tasks
I want it to be interactive	Cheerful welcome Share the purpose Give the big picture Brief description of the 'shape' of the session A positive and encouraging presentational style Well paced, showing awareness of learner's responses Respond to overt challenges in an open, non-judgemental way Watch the body language – your own and that of the participants
I want it to be inclusive	Negotiate a set of group rules to encourage participation Address all sides of the room continually Welcome and value all contributions Involve all participants by actively engaging quiet individuals – to avoid being hijacked by the vociferous Non-threatening and accessible demeanour

In-set 1

Communicating with the emotional brain
An exploration of stress in the classroom with a series of activities and strategies to reduce that stress.
   OHT 1: The three-part (triune) brain
   OHT 2: Effective teachers are skilled at minimising problems
   OHT 3: Learning needs
   OHT 4: Positive correction – a blueprint
   OHT 5: Repertoire of skills

In-set 2

Authority session 1
A dirty word? An exploration of the concept of authority.

In-set 3

Authority session 2
Styles of conflict management.
   OHT 6: Types of poor behaviour
   OHT 7: Making the intervention count
   OHT 8: A context for defusing confrontations

In-set 4

Authority session 3
Characteristics of the authoritative teacher.
   OHT 9: A personal audit

In-set 5

Behaviour issues – session 1
Identifying learning needs within the behavioural curriculum.

In-set 6

Behaviour issues – session 2
The establishment phase – laying the foundations for compliance.
   OHT 10: Teaching about behaviour
   OHT 11: Behaviour strategy framework

In-set 7

Behaviour issues – session 3
The consolidation phase – making the most of it!

In-set 8

Behaviour issues – session 4
The transition phase – dealing with the anxieties

In-set 1
Communicating with the emotional brain

The following information can be used in a number of ways. If the in-sets are to be delivered as a package, then this information must be delivered first.

It does however fit with each of the in-sets, and can be delivered as a preparatory activity in each case. If the in-sets are to be spaced out over a period of time, it may be useful to revisit these pages, prior to each in-set.

Much of the research into the way the brain functions has been done in the last 10 years or so. This could be considered very recent to a profession which operates as it often does in the realm governed by the behavioural theories of people like B.F. Skinner and the cognitive theories of Jean Piaget. Nevertheless, this 'new' knowledge has many powerful messages for us as teachers, and doesn't necessarily invalidate previous beliefs.

We recommend that the in-set presenter should now display **OHT 1** and deliver the following script:

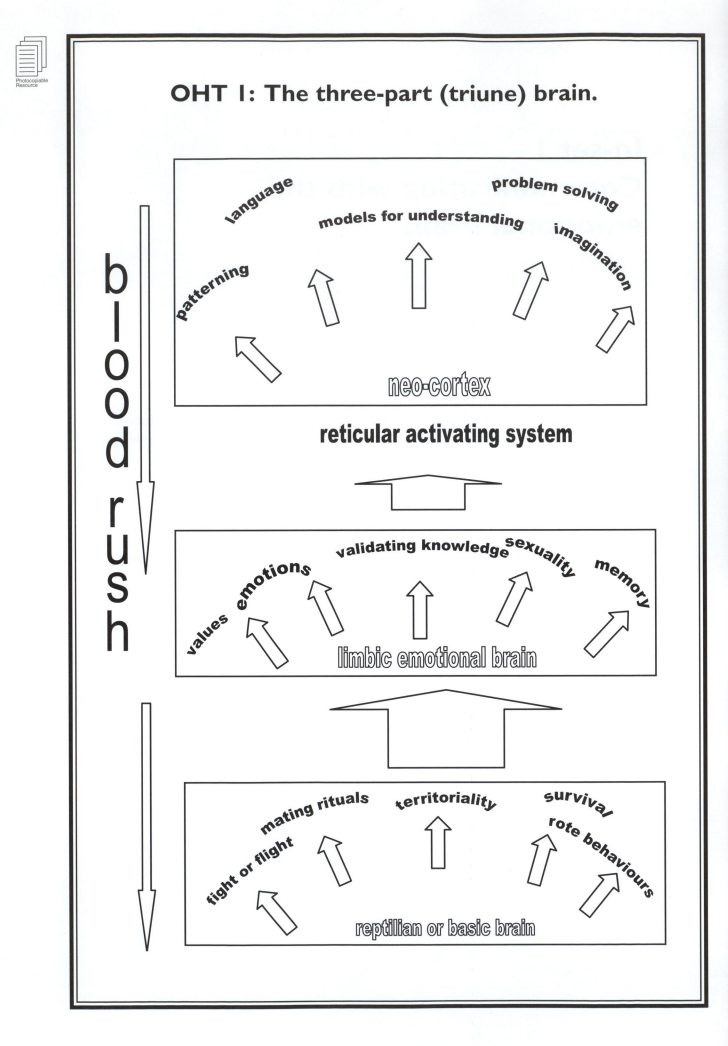

OHT 1: The three-part (triune) brain.

blood rush

problem solving

language

models for understanding

imagination

patterning

neo-cortex

reticular activating system

validating knowledge   sexuality

emotions

values   memory

limbic emotional brain

mating rituals   territoriality   survival/

fight or flight   rote behaviours

reptilian or basic brain

The triune brain

Human beings are in possession of a three-part (triune) brain. The basic, or reptilian, brain, the emotional brain or limbic system, and the cerebral cortex, or neo-cortex.

The basic or reptilian brain governs our primitive responses and survival instincts. If a threat is perceived, whether real or not, the blood supply retreats from the limbic and neo-cortex systems to fuel the reptilian system.

This prepares us for fight or flight, a flood of hormones, adrenalin being the most recognised, arms our bodies for a physical response. Our heart and breathing rates increase in order to pump up the blood supply to our extremities. Our digestive systems slow down and the sphincters in our bodies close down. We are aware of blood pounding in our ears, butterflies in our stomach, clenching of our teeth, and an involuntary tensing of our major muscles. While this response is aroused, the other parts of the brain are unable to function properly until the stress has subsided or been resolved.

Above the reptilian brain is found the limbic system, or emotional brain, which governs memory, values, and obviously our emotions. This part of the brain provides much of the blueprint that makes each of us unique, a distillation of all our experiences, conditioning and stimuli. This part of the brain validates knowledge as useful to us or not.

At the top of the emotional brain is the reticular activating system (RAS), which acts as a filter from the neo-cortex, validating that which resonates with our emotional 'mind-map', and is personally relevant. In front of this lies the cerebral cortex (neo-cortex) which is divided into right and left hemispheres. The neo-cortex is where we use knowledge and concepts to develop skills. This part of the brain governs language and logic. We use our neo-cortex to work out relationships and patterns of meaning. We create personal models for understanding and developing cognitive skills to solve patterns of meaning.

[Now substitute **OHT 2**]

Communicating with the emotional brain is therefore the vital element in managing behaviour and enabling learning to take place. We must therefore search for ways to make our classrooms as low stress and non-threatening as possible, but also to provide high challenge in order to engage the neo-cortex. Those teachers who provide the 'low-stress-high challenge' classroom will undoubtedly have mastered communication with the emotional brain first and foremost.

Easy to say, but not so easy to achieve. Those pupils whose formative experiences, in the home or at school, have been characterised by difficulty, humiliation and failure are very likely to have a poor self-concept. Their values may be incongruent with those of the school. They may have seen only combative behaviour modelled in the home, and their perennial response to authority, in the first instance, is likely to be hostility or denial, or both. These are the youngsters who present the biggest danger to the emotional wellbeing of their teachers.

[Now substitute **OHT 3**]

In considering the functions of each part of the brain, it is possible to translate these functions into needs and to provide some insight into how to fulfil these needs.

[Reference to **OHT 4** and **OHT 5** at this point will give some guidance on useful techniques]

OHT 2: Effective teachers are skilled at minimising problems

Characteristics of a safe learning environment for all

- minimal threat – high challenge

    routines

    resources

    appropriate tasks

    sharing of purpose

- promotion of a positive self-image

    acknowledge student as an individual

    acknowledge individual strengths

    provide appropriate support for individual needs

- encouragement of high self-esteem

    build in early success/reward

    acknowledge and build on that success

    reminders of previous successes

- engagement of positive emotions

    warm welcome

    showing enthusiasm

    showing approval

OHT 3: Learning Needs

The Reptilian (Basic) Brain

- I need to feel safe

    familiar routines

    orderly entrances

    orderly dismissals

    keeping the same seat

    sharing resources safely

- I need to experience success more often than failure

    start with what I can do

    celebrate what I can do

- I need to feel noticed

    say my name

    welcome me

Limbic (emotional brain) system

- I need to feel respected

    as a human being

    as a person of some worth to you

- I need to feel motivated

    use what I remember

    understand my values

    share the purpose of the task

- I need to feel accepted

    my feelings are important too

OHT 4: Positive correction – A blueprint

Positive correction calls into play all the characteristics of the positive teacher, the operation of planned interventions and the repertoire of skills required to make those interventions purposeful, while remaining personable.

The positive teacher

- Remains calm
- Appears confident, detached almost
- Demonstrates vigilance
- Is in control of tone of voice and body language
- Is persistent and assertive

Plans for correction by

- Knowing their students
- Recognising antecedents
- Choosing the language of correction
- Choosing the most effective strategy
- Managing the correction in the least intrusive way

Establishes good beginnings (starts as they mean to go on)

- Greeting students as they arrive
    - Good morning/afternoon, etc.
    - Glad to see you back, are you better? etc.
    - In you come quickly, lots to get through today, etc.
- Naming the rule
    - Taking our jackets off please – thanks!
    - Lining up quietly please – thanks!
    - Sitting down quickly please – thanks!
- Acknowledging the ones who are doing it right
    - Well done Will, you've got your jacket off
    - Thanks Sarah, you've settled quickly today
    - Look at all of you with your jotters out, ready to go!
- Getting attention
    - Responding to a signal, or gesture – OK folks we're ready to go

OHT 5: Repertoire of skills

Non-verbal

- make and maintain eye contact
- positive body language
  - let your demeanour speak for you
  - relaxed stance, hands off hips! Unfold those arms!
  - confident stature
- neutral/cheerful facial expression
- careful gestures
  - the open hand rather than the pointing finger
- close contact
  - respecting personal space

Verbal

- vocal tone – pitch it low
  - reasonable but assertive
  - don't wheedle!
- volume
  - keep it down (if you start loud you've nowhere to go)

Intervention Strategies
(Least intrusive)

- tactical ignoring
- using a mutually understood signal
- move to stand beside/behind the pupil
- say the pupil's name – quietly
- re-frame by distracting or diverting
- give pupil time to comply (by walking away if necessary)

Use your script

- rule reminder
- name . . . pause . . . direction

e.g. 'Will . . . pause (until he's looking at you) . . . I need you to sit down right now please . . . pause. . . . Thanks'

- play the broken record – keep using the above in exactly the same way (3 or 4 times)
- use yes . . . and
- use when . . . then
- consequence reminder
- offer a choice (making sure it's Hobson's!)
  'You have a choice Sarah, you can choose to do what's asked or you can choose . . . whatever consequence you've just stated
- remove the student from the scene (to a pre-arranged and planned location)

Theme: Authority

Contents

In-set 2

- **Session 1**   Authority – a dirty word?

- Activity 1:   Authority – seeking a working definition

- Summary 1

In-set 3

- **Session 2:**   Styles of conflict management – the collaborative model

- Activity 2:   Making the intervention count

- Summary 2

In-set 4

- **Session 3:**   Characteristics of the authoritative teacher

- Activity 3:   Am I insulated against role strain?

- Summary 3:   A personal audit

It is intended that the sessions should be delivered in the order stated since they are intended to address the emotional needs of teachers as learners – What am I supposed to be doing? How am I getting on?

Session 1: Authority – a dirty word?

Notes and introduction to task

Authority has become a rather loaded concept these days, with overtones of the blustering authoritarianism that so many claim had characterised their own education – 'I was beaten every day and it never did me any harm!'

Caricatures of the teaching profession invariably have us portrayed as either Mr Squelch of Beano fame, wearing a heavy scowl, mortar board and gown and wielding a cane, or as a very large, gimlet-eyed harridan, hair scraped into a tight bun with ample bosoms resting firmly on the waistband of her crimplene skirt.

We also appear to be a universally myopic profession since teachers are rarely portrayed without spectacles! Discomfort with this unlovely image has resulted in our shying away from the 'A' word lest we be considered over-bearing and aggressive. The phrase 'Men amongst boys' carried the scornful overtones that teachers were unable to be 'Men amongst men'.

Society's concept of the profession is always going to be rooted in history and therefore rather wide of the mark. Nevertheless society at large conveys authority upon us, demonstrated mainly by holding us responsible for most of society's ills – 'I blame the teachers!' being an oft-repeated mantra, sadly. As a profession we must take up the authority vested in us and assert it, without apology, for the greater good of our pupils and ourselves. Authority as a concept is rarely discussed in schools, there's almost a mysterious and rather nebulous notion that it's something that you possess naturally or you don't. 'Charisma' or presence are often used as substitutes since the results of having either are more visible. There are those teachers whose very appearance in a corridor or classroom is sufficient to cause miscreants to go into 'freeze-frame' and become almost instantly the picture of innocence and compliance. Charismatic figures whose image is so powerful that youngsters rarely misbehave in their classes for fear of losing that person's approval – of being 'out-crowd'. Very often, authority is inherent in the person's position in the school's hierarchy, usually from the head teacher down.

Since this profession is composed of human beings, it follows that within its ranks there will be a normal distribution of temperaments and personalities as in society at large. So, if you're not the head teacher and if your normal persona is rather self-effacing, is it still possible to assume the mantle of authority? Perhaps the answer to that question can be found in an exploration of the manifestations of authority, and in trying to find a way to define what we as a profession feel comfortable with in the exercising of that authority.

Activity 1: Authority – seeking a working definition

You are asked to consider the scenario, as a group, and consider the effectiveness of the options given. Your responses will be recorded on a flip-chart. (Full participation by all will ensure that a wide spectrum of views and responses are represented.) Authority is probably best defined by its manifestations (or lack of same).

> Scenario (supply your own if you wish):
>
> You are on duty in the canteen with other colleagues and you notice a group of older students pushing their way into the queue and intimidating younger students. You only know the name of one of the miscrants.
>
> Do you: (a) Ignore it;   (b) decide to intervene?

If (b): possible options for intervention:

1   Shout out the name of pupil you know
2   Approach the group and then single out the one you know
3   Do you tell him/her to get out of the queue?
4   Do you take the arm of the pupil to get them to leave?
5   Do you approach the group with a colleague?
6   Do you and your colleague remain resolute and calm?
7   They leave – do you thank them for their compliance (however grudging)?
8   Other responses?

As a group, explore the effectiveness of each of these possible options and, using your deliberations from the flip-chart, rank them in order of least to most, then identify those elements within the most successful intervention that points to that conclusion.

Some possible responses

The following are intended for use of the person delivering the in-set. They are not intended to be prescriptive, they are simply fairly typical of those teachers who have taken part in this workshop in the past. Nor is this activity intended to lead teachers on a predictable path towards what they already know. Its intention is to give teachers the opportunity to demonstrate their knowledge of their students and their skills. Also to express their own feelings whilst re-affirming their vital role in the good order of our schools, and above all to enhance confidence.

There are several possible outcomes for each option and a range of effectiveness. The effectiveness of interventions and their consequences can be explored. It is useful to list the possible or likely consequences of each option on a flip-chart.

Choosing option (a) – Ignore it, may have the following outcomes,

- the poor behaviour will prevail
- younger students intimidated
- poor behaviour modelled to younger students
- member of staff feels feeble

(These are not prescriptive lists – teachers will produce many more)

Choosing option (b),

1 *Shout out the name of the pupil you know*, may result in the following responses:

- It's not just me
- You're always picking on me
- That's my name, don't wear it out
- I was here before him (spoken threateningly to a small boy behind him)
- etc, etc

2 *Approach the group and then single out the one you know*, could result in:

- all of the above and
- sniggering of mates
- pupil calling on mates to confirm that he's not queue-jumping

3 *Tell him to leave the queue*, could result in:

- all of the above and
- downright refusal to move
- derisive and hostile behaviour

4 *Take the arm of the pupil to get him to leave*, could result in:

- all of the above and
- 'that's assault, that is'
- 'get your hands off me'
- 'don't you touch me'

Escalation is always a possible response. Pause for a moment to explore how you are feeling at this point – are you angry? Are you shouting? Are you becoming anxious? Are you conscious of an ever-larger audience?

5 *Approach the group with a colleague*, may change the dynamics of the situation:

- this at least gives us the opportunity to say 'Mr/Mrs So and So and I saw you go to the front of the queue' (you are not alone!)
- Mr/Mrs So and So is quite likely to know the name of someone else in the group so the student needn't feel quite so singled out and has less opportunity for feigned indignation
- the youngsters may persist in refusing to leave

6 *Remaining resolute and calm*, can allow you to:

- use the names of the students involved
- re-iterate the school rule as many times as you like
- remind the named students of the consequences of continued refusal
- give the named students the choice of complying with your reasonable request or accepting the consequences

7 *They leave, do you thank them for their compliance?* (However grudgingly performed, and regardless of posturing on their part).

Following up on poor behaviour is a very potent 'marker'. It indicates our refusal to tolerate indiscipline.
  If a delayed consequence is appropriate what possible follow-ups are available?

- seek out student(s) and have a quiet word
- make other staff aware of this particular group
- ask the dinner ladies not to serve queue jumpers
- if this behaviour is repeated make it a consequence that they wait to the end to be served
- other?

Summary I

Can we define authority? Perhaps all we can do is point the way, by a successful demonstration of what we want our personal authority to achieve for us – i.e. compliance – and identify the elements characterised within that. To use our scenario, the maximum effectiveness was achieved by a purposeful intervention conducted in a calm, consistent and resolute manner combined with a thorough knowledge of the likely behaviour of our students.

If we reflect on the least effective options, we can safely predict that if we persist with them, then dinner duty (for example) will continue to be a source of a great deal of anxiety and stress. By thanking the students for their compliance, even though the last emotion you may be feeling is gratitude, you at least enhance the possibility of them being compliant the next time you're on dinner duty.

The authoritative teacher is effective and is therefore:

- self-confident
- high in self-esteem
- assertive
- flexible
- purposeful

Authority as a quality is characterised by

1   compliance
2   respect
3   'clout'

A possible definition of authority could be:

> Authority – comes from giving a purposeful and yet personable
> representation of oneself.

Enhancing one's personal authority is important in one's classroom naturally, but also for those situations in corridors, playgrounds and social areas where the good order of any school is often most at risk. Poor resolution of conflict can result in staff shying away from difficult situations, leaving fewer teachers willing to sign up for those duties that are perceived to be voluntary. This leads inevitably to the escalation of poor behaviour. The corporate support of confident and assertive colleagues in 'perilous' times is absolutely vital, and although inevitably always stressful, is the only road towards our being legitimately 'in charge'.

Session 2: Styles of conflict management – the collaborative model

		The Authority Spectrum		
Conflict				*Resolution*
↓	↓	↓	↓	↓
Competitive	*Avoidance*	*Surrender*	*Halfway House*	*Collaboration*
↓	↓	↓	↓	↓
Aggressive	Allow Disruption	OK, keep doing	OK, you can sit	Recognises
Who are you	(only dealing with	that but don't	and do that as	needs of all
talking to?	the 3 swots in	blame me if	long as you're	concerned
Are you stupid?	the front row)	you get caught	quiet	
Do what I say!				

This diagram clarifies the range of possible responses to behavioural situations which we began to explore in the previous session. Every response has an appropriate time and context when it will be effective. The difficulty is applying the best strategy for the moment. Following on from our previous work, we have probably already discussed the competitive and indecisive responses as being ineffective in the management of conflict. If we look at the next three options we can decide how useful each one will be in defusing a difficult situation:

Surrender: very useful for the here and now;
          very handy if you're tired;
          very useful if you don't know the pupil very well.

This approach, used sparingly and judiciously, can provide much needed peace and quiet. However, it's not very useful for the next time you meet, and not very useful for the next teacher they come across: 'Mr/Miss So and So lets me chew'.

Halfway House: very useful if the rest of the class needs a bit of respite; the activity could be a useful one – it may just be that the pupil prefers it to another.

There will be times when this is the best we can do and is not without positive aspects. However, again it's not so useful if used persistently.

Collaboration: most useful;
          for the here and now;
          for future encounters;
          for one's colleagues.

The collaborative model may be the most useful, but it's also the most difficult to achieve. The collaborative model only works when both parties have access to this style – like our own children, naturally. We know, however, that even the most well-adjusted youngster will come back with a competitive or whining response at any time and for a variety of reasons: mood/age/stage/time of the month/antecedent. Small wonder that those youngsters whose early and continued experiences are characterised by neglect or conflict, or even abuse, or whose values are skewed by years of domestic upheaval, will present a special challenge to the use of the collaborative style in trying to resolve conflict. The chances of them coming back with an aggressive and competitive response are high – their so-called secondary behaviour – their attitude – their physical stance – their body language generally – everything about them sends danger signals to our own reptilian brains.

It's at times like these that the effective teacher falls back on his/her purposeful and personable persona to overcome this by exercising the skills we have mastered. In short, teacher behaviour influences pupil behaviour. Granted, it may not always feel that way when a carefully planned lesson is hijacked by a group of disruptive pupils.

Managing disruption is crucial to a successful or even partially successful outcome. The way we behave is also crucial to our own self-esteem, and to the stress levels experienced when we are challenged by poor behaviour. Managing the the way we behave in order to minimise the behaviour of our pupils is seen as central to good pedagogy, since little learning will take place in a classroom upset by disruption and recrimination. This makes the whole issue of behaviour management a very personal and emotional one, and it is inevitable that we will be upset by poor behaviour.

It is important, therefore, to explore our own personal thresholds of tolerance to recognise mounting stress and to use this awareness to insulate ourselves to some degree. We need to know our own threshold for noise levels, for example – since certain activities are likely to exceed that threshold from time to time. We need to be aware of the level of involvement with our pupils that makes us comfortable. Some of us prefer a detached, rather formal involvement and would find intrusion into that quite stressful.

Others enjoy a high level of personal involvement, using nicknames, having a more tactile approach – pats on the back, ruffling the hair, etc, etc. These teachers find the unexpected and hostile rejection of their approach very stressful indeed.

If we consider an 'involvement' continuum going from remote through to completely involved, we should try to identify that place along the continuum where we can operate comfortably. Knowing our own flashpoints is as vital as recognising the signs of mounting stress in our pupils, if not more so, since as adults we are likely to be better equipped to deal with them.

Group activity: Identifying stressful behaviours

Poor behaviour causes stress in teachers in several ways, by their frequency or by the seriousness of the offence, or by being unexpected. In groups, discuss and identify those behaviours that are encountered daily, those that occur two or three times a week, and those that happen rarely.

Use the chart which follows to record the group's findings.

[For examples, see **OHT 6**]

Problem Behaviours: Frequency and description of behaviour

Daily occurrences

Less/sometimes

Rarely

The person giving the in-set should have a large chart prepared with matching boxes. When the groups re-assemble, they should deliver their findings to the bigger group via the in-set deliverer. The behaviours can then be identified and ranked in a way that separates disruptive behaviours from those involving defiance, and those involving hostility and aggression (although each may contain elements of the other).

The in-set deliverer may prefer to use the findings of the various groups; either way, the purpose is to indicate the escalating stress teachers will experience when being subjected to poor behaviour.

Where we intervene will have a lot to do with our own threshold of tolerance – that is for the individual to decide. Moderation of this decision with colleagues will increase confidence, consistency and effectiveness of the intervention. The nature of the intervention is crucial and will not be successful if we are well into 'stress' mode ourselves.

It is inevitable that there will be stressful interactions during our teaching. Therefore, it is important that we develop a working knowledge of our own responses

OHT 6: Types of poor behaviour

Broadly speaking, there are three main types although each may contain elements of others. This is intended as an exemplar, not as an exhaustive list.

DISRUPTIVE

- Talking out of turn, butting in, calling out
- Lack of correct equipment
- Getting out of their seats
- Playing with objects – cards, toys, radios, etc.
- Making noises, making smells
- Hindering others, defacing other people's work
- Bickering, jostling, borrowing without permission
- Constantly being caught eating
- Inappropriate laughing

DEFIANT

- Ignoring a reasonable request
- Silent non-co-operation – dumb insolence
- Not so dumb insolence!
- Refusing to undertake a task

AGGRESSIVE

- Answering back
- Swearing
- Knocking the furniture about
- Leaving the room, slamming the door
- Threatening violence
- Violence
    Towards another pupil
    Towards the environment
    Towards the member of staff

↓ Escalating stress

to stress including effective techniques to reduce our personal stress level. These will be very individualistic, the suggestions which follow are a starting point for finding our own relaxation techniques. Whatever the technique we use, we need to practise their use and identify the early indicators that we need to use them. Identifying the earliest sign of anxiety buys us time for the relaxation technique to work.

Stress reducers

- pause, don't speak, regather your thoughts
- move away – put some distance between you and the stressor – even if it just involves turning your back briefly
- practise 7–11 breathing
  Breathe in to the count of 7
  Breathe out to the count 11
  Relax neck and shoulders
- Use a prepared script, this may have been developed for this specific situation or may be a personal one which you use when you feel angry.
- Use a prepared exit phrase to avoid getting into a confrontational stand off.

Reflecting on a stressful situation once it's over, either alone, with the offending youngster, or with a sympathetic colleague can be instrumental in reducing that stress. We can then review positive effects of particular actions or phrases which we can use to plan our response for next time. It can also provide an emotional blueprint for the next time we encounter disruption – as we inevitably will.

Activity 2: Making the intervention count

Consider the picture on **OHT 7**. You are encouraged to invent captions for this – feel free (Your captions can be recorded on a flipchart – prizes will be given for the most imaginative!)
   The following notes are for the use of the person delivering the in-set:

The purpose of this section is to place a teacher in a threatening situation on his or her own and to provide possible resolutions that keep at bay the 'reptilian' responses of both participants. (The use of a ludicrous scenario is intended to amuse and relax, and the use of a crocodile is simply a pun on the word 'reptilian').
   The basic question is – 'How do I respond when seriously challenged?' Most responses are very likely to be flippant (this has a role to play in relaxing the participants) but some will contain the kernel of a useful idea.
   We use this to move away from the ludicrous scenario to a more likely one – participants can nominate if they wish.
   The basic underlying message is that one of the school's more 'challenging' pupils is behaving in a threatening way and you have to try to deal with it. (It is very likely that the issue of swearing will come up here and it may be worthwhile to spend some time discussing your own establishment's policy on swearing – distinguishing between the overheard swear word (in response to a frustration), swearing between pupils (signalling an altercation) and in-the-face hostile four-letter invective directed at you personally, referring to your size, age, the shape of your ears/backside, and your pedigree, etc.

OHT 7

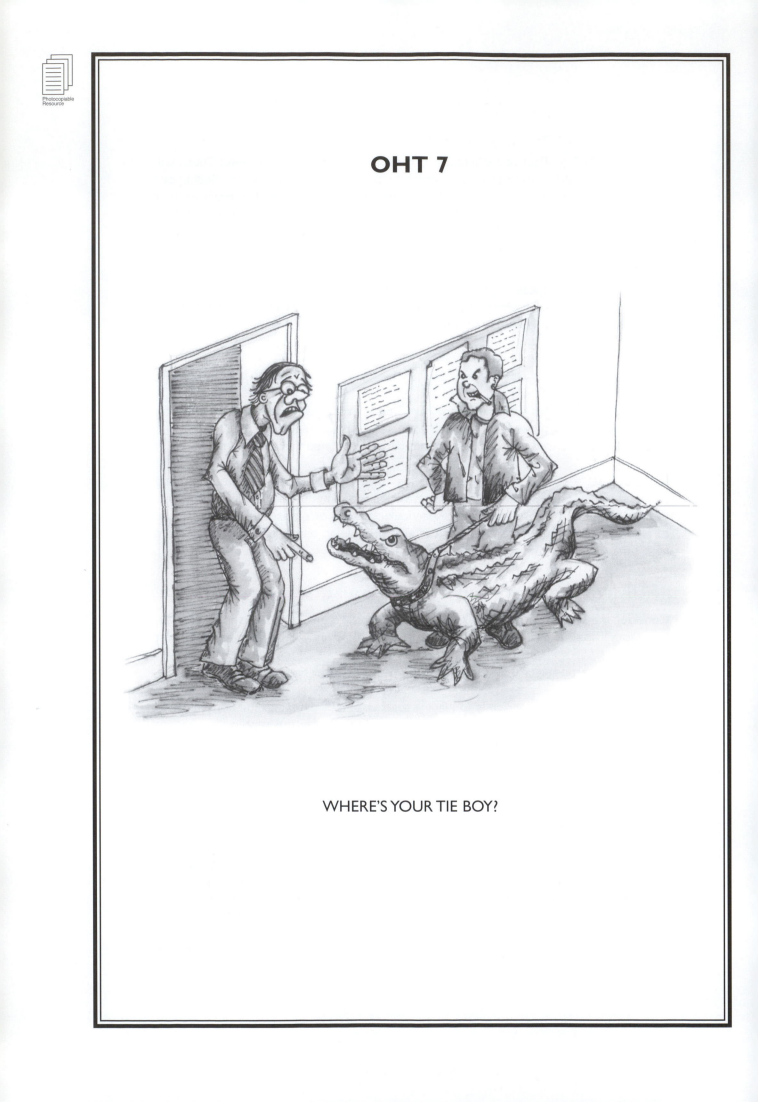

WHERE'S YOUR TIE BOY?

OHT 8: Authority:
A context for defusing confrontations

1   Stay in control of yourself

- don't jump to conclusions
- respond rather than react
- model a relaxed demeanour
  watch your body language
- modulate your tone of voice
- keep the volume down

2   Establish a rapport

- make and keep eye contact – humour
- use a tension release – diversion/distraction
- lead the interaction – reframe

3   Steer clear of a power struggle

- by demanding an admission of guilt (on the spot)
- by concentrating on the behaviour and not the pupil
  don't bring up past misconduct
  don't personalise the issue

4   Keep an escape route open (for you and the student)

- by giving the student a choice

  we can deal with this now or you can come and see me when you've calmed down

  we can deal with this now or you can choose . . . to incur whatever consequences may be available

Inevitably there will be a building of tension during any confrontation. Having a stock of tension releasers in our repertoire of responses is essential. For example,

- humour – often works well, but can backfire when a student is so incensed that humour can actually make the situation worse
- mock shock-horror – surely I didn't see/hear what I thought I saw/heard
- diversion/distraction – try to give the student something else to do
- re-framing the pupil response such as – Pupil repeatedly states, 'I don't f . . . care'. Teacher response repeated as necessary, 'Well I care, and I believe you do too'.

[See **OHT 8**]

Summary 2

Confrontations are always likely when we challenge the behaviour of a hostile student. By responding in a calm and controlled way, we at least open up the possibility of a better resolution. It is more difficult for the student to remain angry and hostile in the face of implacable calm – anger feeds off anger. If we do allow our own reptilian brain to take over, we risk damage to our emotional brain by losing face, as the student shouts back, walks away, completely blanks you out.

Staying outwardly calm is another very powerful 'marker'

- to the offending student
- to anyone watching

If you have kept your 'cool' in the face of provocation you will have enhanced your own feelings of adequacy/potency – hence, although not always resolved to your complete satisfaction, the stress generated by this is likely to subside much more quickly than if the reverse were true. If at the end of such an encounter we ask the question – 'Did anything I did or said make that situation worse?' – and if the answer is 'No, it didn't' we can feel free to move the situation 'up the line' to be dealt with.

We won't always be able to resolve conflict alone. It is important, however, when the dust has settled, to seek out a particular student (in a situation that threatens neither of us) to talk over our last meeting. As the adult in the encounter, we must try to improve any future interactions. Again, this is a powerful 'marker' to a student that we do not necessarily dwell on what has gone before, but that we will not tolerate poor behaviour at any time.

Session 3: Characteristics of the authoritative teacher

The authoritative teacher enters into a situation with the expectation of making a difference. The authoritative teacher is in possession of an armoury, composed of self-confidence backed by a number of tried and tested strategies. The authoritative teacher has a sound knowledge of the likely behaviour of students. The authoritative teacher is aware that there may not be a 'here and now' resolution to a particular situation, but is confident enough to seek out the student at a later date and try to repair and rebuild a relationship.

The authoritative teacher seeks the help of senior colleagues, not in the spirit of weakness, but in the sure knowledge that a joint approach can promote flexibility and purpose – even using the old 'good cop, bad cop' routine – 'I would be ready to contact your parents, but Mr/Mrs So and So (i.e. you) has assured me that this won't be necessary and we can resolve this here and now' – this is a very powerful approach – an antidote to the irascible teacher demanding retribution from a senior colleague who has little or no 'emotional' stake in his/her particular interaction with a student – offering a choice (always the approach to seek), this puts the onus on the student.

The authoritative teacher plans for disruption based on experiences with a group of students, reflects on the likelihood of poor behaviour, and insulates himself against that behaviour. If we know that a particular class presents a particular challenge, we can perhaps plan to minimise that challenge – whether it be from three, four or more particular students, from the location of that class (e.g. a hut with poor facilities), from the time of day (e.g. last two periods on a Friday), or from the aftermath of an assembly, medical inspection, etc., that requires activities that will allow sporadic entry into your class in a directed way.

Minimising stress is very important for teachers, as long as we have tried to establish regimes in our earliest dealings with our students (see *Establishing Routines*), only the most challenging pupils will seek to 'up-end' these regimes. The authoritative teacher remains calm in the face of almost guaranteed provocation – inappropriate language, aggression, irrational responses, evidence of 'moral' differences. Rational behaviour may be the sole province of the teacher since the student presents a completely 'anti-rational' response. The 'Yes, but' student presents a peculiarly intransigent challenge, since their perception of the 'moral' world is likely to be incongruent with the school's regime.

We must seek to brush these differences aside by stating the school's expectations, repeatedly, calmly and with complete confidence. Our example, oft repeated, as moral human beings will only enhance our persona as authoritative teachers.

Activity 3: Am I insulated against role strain?

Do I have authority?

1   Choose your most uncomfortable day of the week
2   List the classes you have on that day
3   As you have listed them, quickly write down a single statement that character-
     ises that class for you, for example:

1 ABC	Very noisy and silly, a large class
3 DEF	William and Sarah!!
4 M 7	Only half the class present (a different half from last week).

Go through that day and list your responses to the following questions:

	Yes	No
Did I feel		
Tense?		
Aggressive?		
Anxious?		
Did I compete with noise?		
Did I issue empty threats?		
i.e. had no effect		
I won't tell you again, repeated endlessly		
Did I invite challenge?		
by ambiguous reprimand		
e.g. Are you deaf, or what?		
Did I become over-emotional?		
Did I feel threatened?		
Did I feel that I taught anything?		

Only you will know if your 'Yes' responses outnumber your 'No' responses, but by doing an exercise like this, it's possible to identify hot spots in your own week. Using the old adage 'fore-warned is fore-armed', it's time to plan for handling the inevitable disruption.

Summary 3: A personal audit

It may be useful at this time to revisit your personal audit on **OHT 9**. It's possible to lose sight of one's objectives when seriously challenged by disruptive behaviour:

- the swaggering, unchastened entrance of a student returning from suspension
- the late entrance of a student fuming from a previous encounter
- a class arriving sporadically from elsewhere, for whatever reason

It's very difficult at times like these not to feel frustrated and to let your frustration show. It's most important to control the entrance into your class by being as calm and business-like as possible; to avoid making any opening remarks; or to allow our frustrated body language to make the situation more difficult to handle.

- Oh, no! You're not back are you?
- I hope you've learned your lesson!
- I don't want any of your messing about.
- What's the matter with you?
- Go out and come in properly.
- Where have you lot been?
- How is it that all these people are on time and you (four/five/six) are not – yet again?

OHT 9: Authority

A personal audit

- Do my students know what is required of them?

- Have I negotiated these behaviours with my students?

- How are these requirements framed?

    Specifically?

    In behavioural terms?

- How do my students know?

    Are they written on the board?

    Are they on a poster on the wall?

    Are they written and pasted inside a jotter?

    Are there pictures on the wall illustrating these behaviours?

- Do I model these behaviours personally?

- Do I have a language of discipline?

    Recognised and valued words of praise and approval

    A well-rehearsed script for limiting disruption

- Are my body language and verbal tone congruent with my verbal message?

- Am I aware of my students' needs? Do I provide appropriate support?

- Do I position myself advantageously in the classroom?

- Do I communicate enthusiasm?

    By being well prepared

    By being brisk and businesslike

These responses may readily spring to our lips but will probably do very little to minimise the disruption and will certainly further delay the onset of the lesson.

The main purpose is to try to establish on-task behaviour as quickly as possible:

- Greet calmly
- Cheerful/neutral facial expression
- Control tone of voice (we sometimes betray our anxiety by a high-pitched, loud or hectoring tone)
- Ignore any posturing on the part of the student
- Seat them as briskly as possible
- Once the bulk of the class is on task, it will be possible to have a quiet word with the individual student – 'I can see that you are very angry Sarah, take a minute or two to calm down. We've got lots to get through this lesson. . . . Thanks!'

It would be naïve and unhelpful to suggest that these strategies will always be effective for all of our students. The level of disaffection found in some of our schools will require a more collegiate approach. If we go back to Activity 3 and we can honestly answer 'No' to most of the questions, then we have done as much as we can alone.

This is when we need to share our experiences with sympathetic and significant colleagues. Such discussions can lead to a de-personalisation of such issues – i.e. William and Sarah are most likely a problem to all the staff they encounter. There's occasionally a colleague who will say that they're fine in their class, which in itself may be a positive to hold on to. It's quite legitimate to ask those colleagues how they manage their students. Case conferences, if they can be convened, can be useful:

- to dispel personal anxieties
- to elicit useful strategies
- to foster feelings of solidarity

The role of parents is discussed elsewhere, but it's safe to assume that they have been kept well informed of the activities of their troublesome youngster. However, the active input of a supportive parent is invaluable. Mutual trust between parent and individual teacher has a very powerful synergy – see *From Policy to Practice*.

What we can do as authoritative teachers is to be aware of conflict situations and to use our personable and purposeful strategies to try to resolve those situations. If we are not particularly successful, according to our own lights, i.e. we have not achieved a significant change in a pupil's behaviour or attitude, as long as we have dealt with that pupil in an honest, calm and non-judgemental way, we have done as much as we should, and we shall have done our best.

Theme: Behaviour Issues

Contents

In-set 5

- **Session 1:**   Behaviour as an issue
- Activity 1a: What's the worst thing?
- Activity 1b: Moderating decisions

In-set 6

- **Session 2:**   The establishment phase – laying the foundations
- Activity 2a: How would we like it to be?
- Activity 2b: The behaviour management framework

In-set 7

- **Session 3:**   The consolidation phase – making the most of it
- Activity 3a: Reframing our view of behaviour
- Activity 3b: Building strategies

In-set 8

- **Session 4:**   The transition phase – dealing with the anxieties
- Activity 4a: Coping with change
- Activity 4b: Easing the change process

Session 1: Behaviour as an issue

Generally when we talk about behaviour we think of inappropriate behaviour. In the context of school behaviour we think of pupil behaviour. If we are to address behaviour management in school we need to consider more closely the range of factors which have significant impact. In order to effect behavioural change then it is helpful to widen our definition. In reality, behaviour is everything we say and everything we do. From this starting point we can consider that our behaviour as adults makes a difference. For example, the way in which you were welcomed to this session, the body language of the person leading the session will have influenced your view of what the session will be like and the way in which you will participate. Our behaviour affects the behaviour of those around us. Think of driving to work in the morning. You are in a traffic queue and let someone join the queue in front of you, often if you watch they will let someone else do the same further down the road. It is your behaviour which has influenced this response. A simpler example is to smile at someone, what response do you generally get?

We concentrate a lot of time in school developing the written and verbal communication skills of our pupils. In our daily lives we rely more and are influenced by non-verbal communication. The learning of these skills tends to happen by chance and through experience. We learn, sometimes painfully, the boundaries of appropriate behaviour for different contexts. As with all learning, we learn at different rates and in different ways. We learn to use our behaviour to defend ourselves in difficult or uncomfortable situations. This may include avoiding situations, interacting in an assertive way, physically placing ourselves near the door for a quick exit. Our behaviour if we are complaining in a shop will be very different to when we are at a gathering of friends and family. We use behaviour to give messages and we build a comprehensive non-verbal vocabulary to communicate our feelings. This can be conscious and unconscious.

Activity 1a: What's the worst thing?

Think of the worst thing which you could be asked to do at this moment in time. Not just something you would not like to do, but the absolute worst thing. Begin to visualise yourself doing the activity. It may involve standing in front of the group, standing on a table etc. You may wish to act out a scene, sing, dance, the possibilities are endless. Time has been allowed for each person to do their particular activity. Ask colleagues how they feel at this point. Flipchart the words suggested which describe their feelings.

For every activity we introduce to pupils in school there will be at least one pupil who feels as you have described. Ask colleagues to explain what lengths they would go to in order to get out of doing that activity. They may leave the room, refuse point blank, feign illness etc.

Flipchart responses

These are all behaviours which we have seen pupils exhibit in school. As adults we have more experience and a more extensive behavioural vocabulary to communicate our feelings. In what ways do we support pupils to learn these skills in school?

Communicating our feelings in an appropriate way is more difficult the stronger the feelings. The organisational structures which exist in our classroom do not lend themselves to individualised behaviour. There is a greater emphasis on group conformity and behaviour expectations based on roles of teacher and pupil.

In groups, assume you have introduced an activity to the class, one pupil feels as you did in our earlier exercise. Consider what opportunities pupils in your class have to express these feelings appropriately in the class situation. Go on to detail how you, as an adult in the class would respond to the pupil. It is often helpful to think of a particular pupil and their likely responses. Feedback to the whole group ideas about successful and appropriate ways which pupils are able to use to communicate the fears and anxieties the task engendered. Record responses on a flipchart. Follow up by identifying ways in which we teach and support pupils to communicate in this way

Activity 1b: Moderating decisions

As we have identified, our behaviour affects the behaviour of others. This is true of adults and children in all contexts. In the school context we have the opportunity to support behavioural learning through giving agreed consistent responses to particular appropriate and inappropriate behaviours. Having the opportunity to agree with colleagues the range of responses appropriate to particular behaviours increases our confidence in responding. The consistency of approach increases the speed of behavioural learning. The discussion also helps to identify factors which affect our decision. There may be good reasons why we react in a specific way to the behaviour from pupil A, but amend this response for pupil B. Raising our awareness of the decision-making process helps to differentiate our response in the same way that we differentiate for curriculum learning.

In small groups consider the following scenarios.

> A pupil hurts another pupil in the playground.
> A pupil hurts another pupil in the classroom.
> A pupil swears at another pupil in the corridor.
> A pupil swears at a teacher in the corridor.
> A pupil refuses to comply with an instruction in the corridor.
> A pupil refuses to participate in a classroom task.

In groups, agree suitable immediate responses to the behaviour. Clarify the factors which will affect your decisions. Consider the pupil involved in the scenario, what behavioural learning needs to take place for the pupil to change their behaviour in the longer term.

Feedback discussion points to the whole group.

Key points for the INSET leader to highlight

There are several factors which influence behaviour, some we can do something about, others on which we have little or no influence. Drawing parallels between adult and child behaviour can give us some insight into the messages which are being communicated. We need to be aware of the opportunities for misinterpretation of non-verbal communication. Every opportunity to clarify the meaning behind a behaviour will increase understanding. By moderating the decisions about the immediate response we approach the situation with a clear plan and confidence that this has been agreed with others. By agreeing a plan out of the situation we are able to formulate a personal script which is not hijacked by our emotions.

By identifying the behavioural learning needed we can work with the pupil to develop 'can do' statements to provide a baseline. From the baseline we can agree targets with realistic timescales. For example, if the 'can do' statement is that the pupil can participate successfully in a class activity for 3 minutes, then the target will be for participation for 5 minutes. Discussion then needs to focus on how will the rest of the time be managed to support the pupils' learning and give them the best possible chance of success.

I have a frightening conclusion

I am the decisive element in the classroom.

It is my personal approach that creates the climate.

It is my daily mood that makes the weather.

As a teacher I possess tremendous power to make a child's life miserable or joyous.

I can be a tool of torture or an instrument of inspiration.

I can humiliate or humour, hurt or heal.

In all situations it is my response that decides whether a crisis will be escalated or de-escalated – a child humanised or dehumanised.

Haim Ginnott, 1972

Session 2: The establishment phase – laying the foundations

[See **OHT 10**]

The establishment phase of the year is usually taken to be from September to November in the academic year. However, establishing the routines and expectations is a process which is often repeated in a variety of contexts in schools. The same principles would apply across these contexts. The establishment phase is associated with feelings of constantly repeating our expectations struggling to impose routines and particular ways of working. It takes a lot of communicating to clarify the way in which we like things to be done in our classroom and our personal priorities. The concept of 'starting again' and new beginning for some of us is an exciting one, for others a tedious ritual before getting on to the real work. As teachers we each have a clear picture in our minds of the behaviours and interactions we wish to encourage in our classroom and school. The establishment phase is the time to lay the foundations for these to become a reality.

By identifying in detail the behaviours and responses we wish to encourage in class, playground, corridor or whole school, we can then plan the learning which needs to take place to support these behaviours. As with all learning it will take place at different rates for each individual and differentiation will be needed to support some individuals.

Using the skills we apply to curriculum learning, we can break down and prioritise the behavioural learning which is needed for the class or school community to work successfully. By drawing parallels between curriculum and behavioural learning it is easier to work with realistic time scales for example, telling someone once what they need to do, being successful is likely to be the exception rather than the rule.

By planning the messages we wish to give pupils about behaviour, we are able to identify ways of modelling and teaching about these behaviours. By identifying the possible vehicles for behavioural learning available we can take account of differentiation, learning styles and revision.

Activity 2a: How would we like it to be?

This can be a small group or individual activity. Agree the context which is to be examined, class, playground, whole school, etc. Describe in terms of observable behaviours what you would like to see in the context. Record these as simple statements. For example,

> Pupils raise their hand if they wish to contribute to a discussion.
> Pupils walk in corridors.
> Pupils use problem-solving approach to conflict resolution.

From those listed, identify three priorities for your school or class.

OHT 10: Behaviour issues: Session 2: Teaching about behaviour, the process

- Decide on the response to behaviour.

- Agree the teaching strategies.

- Highlight the positive.

- Use small-step teaching with realistic expectations.

- Be aware of the effect of our own behaviour.

- Be aware of the effect of the context and environment.

Activity 2b: The behaviour management framework

From our knowledge of how pupils learn and our organisation of curriculum learning we are able to identify principles and practices which can support behavioural learning. For example:

- We cannot make assumptions about previous learning without clear evidence.
- Identifying manageable steps in learning enables progression and motivation.
- Consistency increases the speed of behavioural learning.
- Constructive and positive feedback of progress supports new learning.
- Involving learners in targets, rewards and sanctions improves motivation.
- Taking account of learning styles increases speed of learning and motivation.

These are principles and practices which we regularly use in curriculum teaching and learning. The same principles can be applied to behavioural learning.

In groups, identify ways in which the behaviours from the previous activity can be taught and positively reinforced. For example, clearly display the positively phrased rule in the class, reinforce through specific praise for individuals who comply. Do not accept responses from pupils not raising their hands. Teach specific conflict resolution process, display around school, support and reward evidence of use of process. The conflict resolution process may be centred on a stepped process such as:

1   Each person says what they think happened
2   Mediator retells the main points
3   Those involved suggest solution
4   Conflict agreed to be resolved.

For the previous discussion we are aware that there are many influences on behaviour. Behaviour management is not an exact science. Therefore it is useful at this stage to consider times at which the rule will not apply, such as not raising hands to speak during small group discussion. Decide how these exceptions will be communicated to pupils.

For the majority of pupils these messages and expectations, clearly communicated, will be sufficient to support their behavioural learning and appropriate responses within school.

- The basic behaviour strategies are the same for everyone.
- Each additional level is then differentiated.

[See **OHT 11**]

Using this behaviour framework we can clarify the behaviour management strategies and approaches which we will employ with all pupils to support appropriate behaviour. These strategies will be taught and reinforced mainly during the establishment phase.

These strategies will form the basis of the behaviour framework. As groups and individuals identify themselves as needing further behavioural teaching, strategies can be differentiated.

OHT 11: Behaviour issues: Session 2
Behaviour strategy framework

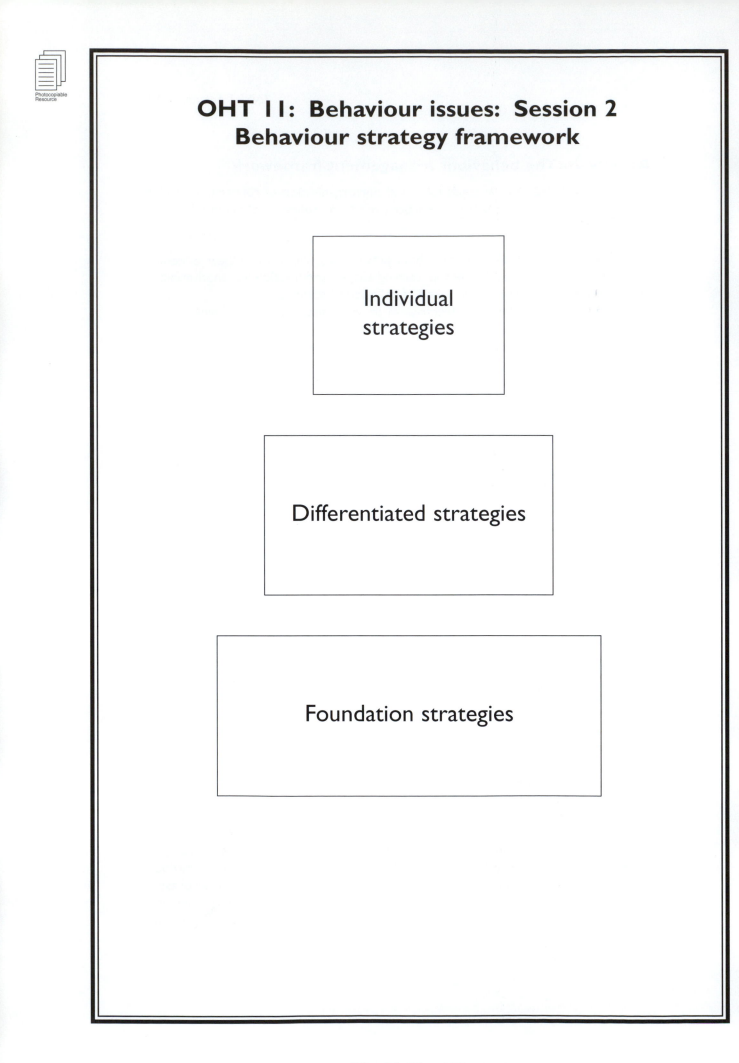

Individual strategies

Differentiated strategies

Foundation strategies

Session 3: Consolidation phase – making the most of it

The consolidation phase is the stage when the majority of pupils have assimilated the necessary behavioural learning to respond appropriately in the majority of contexts. It is also the stage when we are best able to predict patterns of behaviour from individual pupils. We must not forget that pupils by this stage are best able to predict our patterns of behaviour too.

It is an appropriate time to revisit the behaviour strategies employed during the consolidation phase with pupils to reflect on progress. This can easily be done through the use of 'can do' statements. For example, as a class we can settle to a task within 10 minutes. Such statements can be constructed considering whole school, whole class, groups or individuals as appropriate.

Activity 3a: Reframing our view of behaviour

With a colleague identify five 'can do' statements for a class/group/individual with whom you are involved. For example, year 3 can settle to a given task within 10 minutes. Year 1 can move around the classroom appropriately to collect equipment during activities fifty per cent of the time.

Key points for INSET leader to highlight

Be as specific as you can, where possible include a time element as in the example.

As adults in school we regularly identify what pupils can do in a curriculum context to focus teaching strategies to progress new learning. Behaviour is more often identified in the negative which does not identify teaching and learning required.

Feed back to the whole group a selection of the 'can do' statements. This may lead to additions or further detail being considered. There may also be opportunity to compare the response of groups/individuals in different contexts.

Activity 3b: Building strategies

Use the 'can do' statements to identify the learning targets and teaching strategies which will enable progress. For example, if class/group can settle to task within 20 minutes, our target could be to reduce this to 15 minutes. The teaching strategies may include:

1 feedback to class that present achievement level is 20 minutes
2 identify what needs to be done to settle to task
3 identify any specific difficulties and possible solutions
4 give regular feedback about progress
5 share the record keeping (i.e. the number of minutes written on the board)
6 reflect on the times when it improves to identify why it was quicker.

Key points for INSET leader to highlight

Consider the teaching strategies in relation to your knowledge of the learning styles of the pupils involved. For example can we use visual display, rehearsal, demonstration and verbal explanation to support learning?

The priority is to give pupils the best possible chance to succeed.

Session 4: Transition phase – dealing with the anxieties

Any change, however small, can give rise to anxiety and fears. This is true of both adults and children, of course. In the academic year, the major changes take place during the final term but smaller changes from activity to activity, classroom to playground etc, also cause problems. By their very nature transitions provide opportunity for anxiety, uncertainty and lack of structure. In behavioural terms, established routines are challenged and boundaries pushed to confirm or deny security. Individuals feel vulnerable and unsure of how to respond, as well as less able to control behaviour because of the increased emotional element.

Activity 4a: Coping with change

It is often helpful to draw parallels between pupil experience and our own. Consider the most recent major change you experienced, for example new job, new house. Identify the range of feelings you experienced. Some will be related to the particular change, others generic to experiencing a transition. Discuss and list the feelings which are generated by change. Consider if there are any differences if the change is imposed or chosen.

Record the feedback to the whole group on a flipchart.

In school. transitions are a major part of life, from activity to activity, class to class, class to playground, year group to year group, teacher to teacher, etc. In each of these situations, there are issues for both pupils and adults.

Activity 4b: Easing the change process

Review and reflect on the feelings you identified related to transitions. In a small group, share ideas about what can make transitions easier. For example, clear information about what will happen, details of when things will happen, the order in which they will happen, who will be involved.

Identify ways in which these strategies can be employed in the school context. For example, giving time warnings to the end of task, explaining the order in which events will take place, clarifying expectations for specific activities, liaison between year groups, primary/secondary infant/junior schools.

Key points for INSET leader to highlight

Often strategies are employed to address the major transitions, e.g. primary to secondary but less notice is taken of daily transitions which may cause pupils significant difficulty. These smaller transitions will have an on-going effect on behaviour. Returning to the Behaviour Management Framework (Session 2, Activity b) and ensuring that the foundation strategies include addressing the issues raised by transitions can be helpful.

Suggested further reading

Goleman, D. (1996) *Emotional Intelligence*, London: Bloomsbury Publishing

Hare, W. (1993) *What Makes a Good Teacher*, Winnipeg: The Althouse Press.

Long, R. and Fogell, J. (1999) *Supporting Pupils with Emotional Difficulties*, London: David Fulton Publishers.

Milner, P. and Carolin, B. (eds)(1999) *Time to Listen to Children*, London: Routledge.

Morrison, T. (1993) *Staff Supervision in Social Care*, Brighton: Pavillion Publishing.

Rogers, W. A. (1990) *You know the Fair Rule,* London: Financial Times/ Prentice Hall

Rogers, W. A. (1992) *Managing Teacher Stress*, London: Pitman Publishing

Visser, J. and Rayner, S. (eds) (1999) *Emotional and Behavioural Difficulties*, Lichfield: Qed Publishers.

Warden, D. and Warden, C. (1997) Teaching Social Behaviour, London: David Fulton Publishers.

Index

Action plan, 15, 16, 49, 50, 53
Authority, 68, 69, 72

Behaviour management forum, 13, 14, 49, 50
Behaviour management plan, 10, 20, 24, 29, 31
Blitzing, 50
Body language, 17, 79, 83

Calendar, 15, 21, 23, 38
Caricatures, 69
Charisma, 69
Comfort zone, 29, 58
Community education, 12
Communication, 8, 17, 18, 24, 32, 33, 54, 55, 86
Consolidation phase, 15, 21, 41, 43, 46, 47, 93

Discipline policy, 6, 8, 9, 10, 16
Displays, 34

Elton Report, 30
Emotional brain, 3, 5, 30, 50, 61
Establishment phase, 15, 21, 24, 26, 28, 31, 37, 38, 43, 48, 49, 89
Exclusion, 2

Firefighting, 29
Furniture, 34

Ginnott, Haim, 88

Intervention, 77

Language, 24
Limbic emotional brain, 4, 5, 62

Meetings, 11, 44
Motivation, 43, 46, 91

Neo-cortex, 4, 62

Parent's evenings, 11
Piaget, Jean, 61
Policy, 7
Practice, 7

Reptilian brain, 4, 5, 62
Reticular activating system, 4, 62
Rewards, 14, 32, 43, 45, 47, 49, 50
Rogers, Bill, 15

Senior management team, 13, 14, 16, 52
Skinner, B.F., 61
Social skills, 17
Social work, 12
Spirit lifters, 52
Stress-busting, 40, 52, 56, 77
Success, 38, 43, 44, 45
Summer school, 17
Support, 38, 39, 40, 43
Suspension, 9
Swearing, 9, 77

Tantrums, 31
Target-setting, 44, 45
Transition phase, 15, 21, 50, 94
Triune brain, 3, 62, 63